PRA...

Finding Your Walden

"In these overwhelming times, Jen Tota McGivney gives us the Thoreau we desperately need—a friend who wishes us well, a life coach whose experiment in intentional living in the mid-19th century offers a lifeline in the early 21st. McGivney debunks the view of Thoreau as an irascible hermit, showing us a devoted friend and family member who wanted to make the most of his one, short life. Thoreau's lifelong efforts to rethink economics, to periodically retreat from society, to embrace his misfit status, and to build a life defined by purpose and joy are not confined to literary history but, as McGivney shows us, connect to a broad movement of (extra)ordinary people who continue to try the experiment of living. As she teases out the lessons Thoreau learned on the shores of Walden Pond, McGivney draws on dozens of stories that show how people in our own time have escaped quiet desperation and began to live the lives they imagined. So can we."

—John J. Kucich, PhD, president of the Thoreau Society, professor of English, Bridgewater State University

"Jen McGivney's clear and charming book brings Thoreau's teachings into our modern world of noise and distraction, and grapples with the big questions, mainly: What kind of life do we want to live?"

—Tommy Tomlinson, author of
Dogland and *The Elephant in the Room*

FINDING YOUR WALDEN

How to Strive Less, Simplify More,
& Embrace What Matters Most

JEN TOTA McGIVNEY

HAMPTON ROADS

This edition first published in 2025 by Hampton Roads Publishing,
an imprint of Red Wheel/Weiser, LLC
With offices at:
65 Parker Street, Suite 7
Newburyport, MA 01950

Sign up for our newsletter and special offers by going to
www.redwheelweiser.com/newsletter

Cover by Sky Peck Design
Interior by Timm Bryson, em em design, LLC
Typeset in Weiss

ISBN: 978-1-64297-063-0
Library of Congress Cataloging-in-Publication Data
available upon request.
Printed in the United States of America
IBI
10 9 8 7 6 5 4 3 2 1

For Jimmy, of course

Here is life,
an experiment to a great extent untried by me.

—HENRY DAVID THOREAU, *Walden*

CONTENTS

INTRODUCTION

In These
Precedented Times . . .

[Walden] is a document of increasing pertinence;
each year it seems to gain a little headway,
as the world loses ground.
—E. B. WHITE

History may not repeat, but it often rhymes, or so Mark Twain (might have) said. Our times rhyme with the times of Henry David Thoreau as neatly as a Dr. Seuss story.

If we could span a 175-year divide to pull up a chair beside Thoreau, we could chat all day with him. We'd talk about the pros and cons of belonging to generations when technology advanced more in our lifetimes than during previous centuries, revolutionizing how people lived, worked, and communicated. We'd gripe about dirty partisan politics, fanned by companies profiting from the divide. We'd talk about the rich getting richer, and the rest of us just working harder. We could even discuss how living during a pandemic compelled us to question our priorities and our relationship to work.

And yet! And yet "In these unprecedented times . . ." has become a cliché in news, in ads, in conversations. Why do we feel so alone in history? I believe it's beyond coincidence that our loss of historical connection has happened as fewer people read classic literature. These books didn't become classics just by getting old. They did because they're timeless stories about how people got through the chaos of life and how we might, too. These stories can give us company during these very precedented times. And we can find plenty of company in Thoreau's 1854 masterpiece,

Walden; or, Life in the Woods. In it, Thoreau looks at his fast-changing, conflict-ridden, overpriced world and wonders: Do I really need all this stuff? When should I take a job— and when should I leave one? What's my duty as an ethical citizen of a less-than-ethical world? How can I live a good life amid [insert hand-sweeping gesture] all of this?

We get it. We live during a similar philosophical reckoning. We now question assumptions that we barely noticed we even had—about what we need, what we don't—and we search for a new way, a simpler way. Thoreau's writing points us toward this way. He's proof that we're not as isolated as we feel, that another generation navigated something like this already and left guidebooks behind to help.

It's not just our generation that resists reading old books, however. Thoreau lamented that, even during his lifetime, not enough people hit the classics for inspiration. In *Walden*, Thoreau made a solid case to seek insight within the bindings of old books:

> How many a man has dated a new era in his life from the reading of a book. The book exists for us perchance which will explain our miracles and reveal new ones. These same questions that disturb and puzzle and confound us have in their turn

occurred to all the wise men . . . and each has answered them, according to his ability, by his words
and his life.

No book has dated a new era in my life like *Walden* has. No
author has answered the questions that disturb and puz-
zle and confound me like Thoreau has. I've toted my dog-
eared, underlined Everyman's edition with me for decades
like a talisman. *Walden* has changed my life, and I'll show
you how it might change yours, too.

Not Just Less Stuff, Better Stuff

When people distill *Walden* down to a tattoo or bumper
sticker, it's usually his most famous line: "Simplify, simplify."
But it's easy to miss what Thoreau simplified for. He didn't
simplify to have and to do less; he simplified to have and
to do more of what mattered. To trade up, he pared down.

Contrast that to life today. We're drowning in a culture of accumulation. We never quite earn enough. Have
enough. Do enough. We never quite *are* enough. We focus
on what's next, believing that when we earn/have/do/be-
come a little more, we can finally relax. We don't, of course,
because then there's more to earn/have/do/become. There's
a term for this: lifestyle creep. In its advanced stages, we

bury so much of that good stuff we started with—our curiosity, our joy, our us-ness—beneath the weight of expectations of the person we hope to become without realizing the value of the person we've been all along.

When we live in an era that moves so quickly, it's hard to pause long enough to wonder if we prioritize the right things, pursue the right goals. This is by design. The lifestyle that we've been sold lines others' pockets more than it enriches the quality of our days. We're told that work should be our passion, which makes overtime feel more like a sacrament than a sacrifice. Social media transforms our time—our lives!—into engagements to be monetized. Consumerism makes everything available for purchase: status, beauty, health, even youth. New devices are sold to streamline our lives, but they distract us from them. "Our inventions are wont to be pretty toys, which distract our attention from serious things," Thoreau wrote.

As a transcendentalist, Thoreau believed that people are innately good and that we are born with an intuition that will guide us to the right decisions if we listen to it. It's our job not to drown our intuition beneath the demands of a society that doesn't have our best interests at heart. "I am convinced, both by faith and experience, that to maintain one's self on this earth is not a hardship but a pastime, if we live simply and wisely," he wrote.

It's a crucial time to seek wisdom in this philosophy. "A cardiologist, endocrinologist, obesity specialist, health economist and social epidemiologists all said versions of the same thing: Striving to get ahead in an unequal society contributes to people in the United States aging quicker, becoming sicker and dying younger," according to a story in *The Washington Post*.[1] While many of these strivers have no choice (people who work multiple jobs to put enough food on the table), others do so voluntarily. It's what we're conditioned to do—to never stop climbing—as success perpetually awaits on the next rung. But this isn't the only version of success. It's worthwhile to question what this society asks of us and what we're willing to give it. And no writer questions that better than Thoreau.

Thoreau encourages us to define success for ourselves— to recognize when we can strive a little less and live a little more. He teaches that there can be more power in letting go than adding on.

This is a message of radical hope. Thoreau insists that life has so much joy to offer if we live intentionally and prioritize wisely. How we choose to live can become our greatest art:

I know of no more encouraging fact than the un-questionable ability of man to elevate his life by a conscious endeavor. It is something to be able to paint a particular picture, or to carve a statue, and so to make a few objects beautiful; but it is far more glorious to carve and paint the very atmosphere and medium through which we look, which morally we can do. To affect the quality of the day, that is the highest of arts.

Thoreau had one mission: to encourage people to pause, to notice, to question. He points to the beauty of what's in front of us, if only we'd see it: "Heaven is under our feet as well as over our heads." To do that, we must consider if a better way of living exists, even if it's one that no one has thought of yet—or, perhaps, *especially* if it's one that no one has thought of yet.

A Tough Read and a Hard Sell

I admit that *Walden* isn't an easy read. The language is dated. Thoreau's dad jokes have aged from corny to inscrutable. (The guy loved a pun.) Suggesting that someone unwind after a hard day with 19th-century literature is a big ask. We're inundated with words all day: emails, articles, texts— it never stops. The problem isn't that we don't read; it's that we read so much that it feels hard to relax by reading even more. When we skip the great books, however, we miss so much—enjoyment and challenge, sure, but we also miss the chance to meet someone who lived centuries ago and think, "Hey, you too?"

After years of trying and failing to get my friends to read *Walden* (I'm fun at parties), I changed tactics. I pitched a story to *Success* Magazine about how the messages of *Walden* can improve our work lives. Pitching a story about Thoreau to *Success* is like pitching a story about barbecue to *Vegetarian Times*. Thoreau's reputation isn't exactly about crushing it in the office. But it worked. The grateful reader emails I received proved that Thoreau is the man for our age, even if *Walden* might not be the reading material for our time.

I've expanded that concept here. I've turned Thoreau's writings into a philosophy of 21st-century intentional living. In this book, you'll learn why experts—from physicians to career coaches to psychologists—support Thoreau's ideas as inspiration for living well. Alongside them, you'll read about people who live those ideas today, who make big and little acts of everyday resistance against the demands of the status quo. This book isn't a step-by-step guide to intentional living but a choose-your-own adventure. It shares all kinds of ideas, from major life-upending experiments to minor lifestyle tweaks. What does it look like to live a Thoreauvian life? For one couple in this book, it looks like selling their home to fund a year-long sabbatical in Bali with their kids to rediscover what they need (and what they don't) and who they are (and who they aren't). For some, it looks like downshifting to a four-day workweek or adopting a digital sabbath. For one woman, it simply looks like downsizing her clothes into a capsule wardrobe that declutters her closet and streamlines her routine. Each person has applied creativity, simplification, and joy to the experiment of life and offers inspiration on how we might, too. If you take one thing from Thoreau and the people in this book, take this: Life is, after all, an experiment. No one can tell us how to do it; it's something we need to figure out as we go. And if our life looks suspiciously like the lives of the people around us, we might be doing it wrong.

Our Friend Henry

For the past seventy-five years, *Walden* has sat on the shelf and in the curricula beside *The Catcher in the Rye* as anthems of adolescence, books teachers assign to feign credence to youthful idealism before moving onto the real texts. Then, we become respectable, cynical adults who accept the way things are. We get a real job, we buy uncomfortable clothes, and we give up idealism and Henry David Thoreau.

I never gave Thoreau up.

I first met Thoreau at fourteen, shortly after my family moved to Northern Virginia. Our introduction couldn't have been better timed, as I became a bewildered witness to Washington, DC–area life. There, success looked like long commutes, stressful jobs, and little time to enjoy what was being worked for. I'd hear adults compete over who had it worst—whose drive was the longest, whose job was the most bureaucratic—but I rarely heard them consider other ways. Some people didn't seem to mind their own misery; a few seemed to boast of it. Thoreau was the first adult to tell me that he didn't find this arrangement very attractive either, that the way things are is not the way things have to be. He taught me that success didn't have to involve a fancy office and a big house and that the goal didn't have to be to acquire as much as possible: stuff, money, accolades. Success could look like contentment.

Holding *Walden* was like holding a treasure map. Thoreau and I were going to think our way out of this jam. We've spent every year since figuring out just that: How can I make a good living while living a good life?

Since then, Thoreau's become my life coach. Almost every major decision I've made—which degree to pursue, when to accept (or quit) a job, where to live—starts with an imaginary huddle with Thoreau. He challenges me to doubt myself, just enough, to wonder: Will this decision make me become more fully me, or will it just make me a little more like everyone else?

This may sound crazy to people who don't love *Walden* (yet), but there's a reason this book is so beloved, staying continuously in print since 1862. Thoreau accomplishes something special (and personal) with *Walden*. The subject of almost every book is a fictional character, a historical figure, or the author themself. In *Walden*, however, the subject is you. "Walden is as personal as a letter from a close friend," wrote Philip Van Doren Stern in *The Annotated Walden*, "a friend who wishes you well."

Like me, many Thoreau fans have an oddly personal relationship with an author who lived long before they were born. I spoke with Brent Ranalli, a Thoreau scholar and impersonator. When people visit the replica cabin at Walden Pond, Ranalli sometimes greets them, wearing an authentic outfit and ready to answer their questions as Thoreau himself. I asked Ranalli how visitors interact with him, what he sees in their eyes. "A lot of people already have a relationship with Thoreau," he told me. "There are a lot of people who really admire him and who think of him as a friend."

Thoreau has many friends. The Thoreau Society is the largest and oldest organization dedicated to an American author, filled with many nonacademics who simply adore the guy. This isn't normal. Most literary societies consist mostly of PhDs pursuing research. But some regular folks, like me, consider Thoreau as a guru of intentional living and want to meet others who do, too. Others are drawn to his environmentalism or scientific research. There's just something special about Thoreau. "He speaks to his readers wherever they are," Ranalli said. "There's always been this enthusiasm for him."

It's a lonely and overwhelming time, and Thoreau is just the friend we need to help us through it. Thoreau's words cut a path toward a more fulfilling, more peaceful life. We just need to make a stop at a cabin along the way.

Correcting the Myth

As we start, it's important to correct a misconception about Thoreau. He didn't live at Walden Pond to turn his back on the world. He went there to learn how to live better in the world when he got back to it. His two years in that cabin—which was just a mile and a half beyond town—were the only years he lived alone. The rest of his life was surrounded by a close family and good friends. Thoreau's goal at Walden Pond was to go just far enough away, just long enough away, to hear his own thoughts. He wanted space to answer the two big questions: What really matters? And what doesn't?

Everyone I know is trying to answer those questions now.

But first, a word of warning and apology: *Walden* doesn't answer those questions. Neither does this book. *Walden* provokes more questions. So does this book.

Thoreau didn't write *Walden* to tell people to live alone in a cabin in the woods. He wrote *Walden* to share the ideas that his time in the woods inspired, to encourage people to challenge their mode of living and to wonder how to make life a little better, a little easier, a little happier. How each of us does this will look different from our neighbors and friends, if we live according to our values. The message of the following pages isn't to send you off to a cabin in the woods. The message is to find your questions, find your answers.

Find your Walden.

Henry David Thoreau

The Make-Up Class

If it's been a while since you've read *Walden* (or if you skipped that book in English class—I won't tell), start here.

Who Was Henry David Thoreau?

Thoreau was a writer who lived from 1817 to 1862 in Concord, Massachusetts. He was part of the transcendentalist movement, which proclaimed that people are inherently good (think the opposite of original sin) and that they should trust their intuition rather than conform to society. Thoreau's neighbors were a who's who of the movement: Ralph Waldo Emerson, Margaret Fuller, Nathaniel Hawthorne, and Louisa May Alcott.

Transcendentalism was more than writing, however. In maintaining the theme of individual freedom, transcendentalists fought against slavery and advocated for women's rights. For example, Thoreau was an operative on the Underground Railroad and an outspoken abolitionist.

What Is Walden About?

Walden is Thoreau's book about his two-year, two-month, and two-day experiment at Walden Pond. It was part working sabbatical, part quarter-life crisis. When Thoreau was twenty-eight, burned out from job frustrations and bill paying, he built a cabin by a pond and spent the next couple years writing, gardening, and wondering why the world was such a difficult place to find contentment. *Walden* is Thoreau's account of what he learned during that time as he looked at the world from a distance while seeking a better way to live in it when he returned.

Why Is Walden Considered a Classic?

Walden speaks to the self-questioning that's necessary for each of us to find our own way: When should I follow the crowd, and when should I trust my gut? What's the right balance between work and fun, between solitude and connection? Nearly 175 years later, these questions have only grown more complicated and urgent.

Also, *Walden* is a beautiful piece of writing, whether Thoreau ponders job satisfaction or describes the peace of the woods at sunrise. It's impossible to read the book without underlining passages. Also, one less-appreciated feature of Thoreau's is his humor: While his word play doesn't always translate well now, Thoreau was a pun machine who took dad jokes to a new level.

Was Thoreau Famous When He Was Alive?

Somewhat. If someone followed transcendentalism, they knew Thoreau's name. He gave lectures throughout the region, and he published stories in magazines like *The Atlantic Monthly*. His celebrity grew, ironically, when he retreated to Walden Pond. Word got out about a transcendentalist writer who lived alone in a homemade cabin in the woods, and he captured unintentional publicity. Much of the publicity wasn't kind; people didn't like the idea of someone who refused to follow the unspoken rules of society. That, however, brought him admirers of fellow misfits who wanted to defy those rules, too.

While he was a leading figure of the transcendentalist movement, Thoreau wasn't the household name then that he is now. In fact, his first book was a commercial flop that landed him in debt and caused many publishers to pass on his next book. (What a mistake for them, as that next book was *Walden*.)

Did Thoreau Really Make His Mom Do His Laundry While He Lived at Walden Pond?

Oh boy. The laundry controversy. If you're unfamiliar, this is an issue that some people use to discredit Thoreau's messages entirely, as if Thoreau ever claimed to live a life of total solitude and self-sufficiency. (He did not.) It centers on this line in *Walden*: "washing and mending . . . for the most part were done out of the house, and their bills have not yet been received." Let's dig in to see what the fuss is about.

Interpretation 1: Thoreau brought his laundry home. If so, it was likely not washed by his mother but by her employees. Thoreau's mother ran the family house as a boarding home, one that Thoreau supported. He contributed to the home's down payment and assisted in its construction, helped her entertain guests, and paid rent while he lived there. Thoreau was hardly a freeloader. (I'd throw my laundry in, if I were him.) Back then, washing clothes by hand was an all-day affair, and many middle-class families outsourced the task, much like how most people today don't tailor their own clothes.

Interpretation 2: Thoreau did laundry "out of the house" by washing it in the pond. In his excellent essay on the "laundry sneer," Brent Ranalli quotes a woman who recalled meeting Thoreau: "I think his laundry work must have been his own personal care. No washerwoman would have risked her laundry reputation and turned off such work."[1] While not high praise of Thoreau's personal habits, it supports the pond theory.

A final word: Does it matter? What other writer has been discredited due to their laundry habits? I doubt that Emerson—Mr. "Self-Reliance" himself—was ever elbow-deep in suds. Mark Twain or Henry James? Not a chance. Not many 19th-century writers inspire the backlash that Thoreau inspires. To me, it's proof that Thoreau strikes a 21st-century nerve. He forces us to ponder hard questions (Could we be doing life a bit better? Are we more conformist than we care to admit?), and it might be easier to poke holes in his arguments than in our own.

Why Do You Love This Guy so Much?

Thoreau advocated for himself—his happiness, his ideas, his quirkiness—and advocated for the rights of others. He never accepted the excuse of that's just the way things are. Thoreau cared more about living a life that met his own approval than bending it to gain the respect of others. I can't think of a better way to live. Each time I read *Walden*, Thoreau challenges me to maintain the day-to-day fight for my happiness and ideals, to be willing to take a risk, to stand apart. My hope is that you'll love him, too.

Know the True Cost of Things

We pay with more than money.
We pay with our life.

The cost of a thing is the amount of what I will
call life which is required to be exchanged for it,
immediately or in the long run.
—HENRY DAVID THOREAU

Real happiness is cheap enough,
yet how dearly we pay for its counterfeit.
—HOSEA BALLOU

I love Henry David Thoreau. I've spent my life nearly obsessed with him. But I get it: He can be a tough read. As we begin, I suggest this: When you read Thoreau, think Bruce Springsteen. It helps to think of Thoreau as not just a 19th-century transcendentalist writer but also as the super-nerdy Boss of his day. One of the two is far cooler and dreamier than the other—and we all know who—but they're both rock and roll in their own ways. Thoreau and Springsteen are both poets of the working class who look out onto the ways of the world and think, *Nah, we regular folks can do better than this.*

In *Walden*, Thoreau provokes us to do better. You can distill his philosophy into one sentence, one that upends the system we were born into: "The cost of a thing is the amount of what I will call life which is required to be exchanged for it, immediately or in the long run." We spend more than our money, Thoreau reminds us; we spend our time, our energy. We spend our life. Each purchase requires not only the dollars we trade for it but also the time and energy we use to earn those dollars. And with a little distance, we see that many of the ways we spend our money, time, and energy are—frankly—dumb.

With this one sentence, Thoreau redefines cost and profit. A nice house in the suburbs might not be worth the hour it takes to commute from it nor the mortgage that keeps its owners locked into jobs they hate. A high-paying career that pads the bank account but robs someone of joy and hobbies may come with more expense than profit. It might be worth trading the payment on a luxury car for the time it takes to earn it. The world tells us the literal price of things; Thoreau reminds us that it's up to us to remember their cost.

I've created a term to describe this: Waldenomics. Waldenomics is a personal economic model that puts money in its periphery but maintains profit as its goal. If we trade in life, how's our return on investment?

Somehow, *Walden* has gained the reputation of being a book that shuns the ideas of wealth and success. Not so. The book redefines wealth and success. It's no mistake that the first (and longest and most quoted) chapter of *Walden* is titled, "Economy." Thoreau's making a pun here, one of his many, many puns. In one meaning, "economy" describes the economics of life, the hard facts and figures. In the other meaning, "economy" refers to scarcity, paring down to the basics. In this chapter, Thoreau tells us that his Walden Pond experiment is meant to learn how to live well with less: "My purpose in going to Walden Pond was not to live cheaply nor to live dearly there but to transact some private business with the fewest obstacles" and "I have thought that Walden Pond would be a good place for business."

At Walden Pond, Thoreau investigated the business of life. He realized that the American way left too many behind, convincing people they could beat a dealer with a stacked deck. Instead, he built a cabin, put some distance between himself and others, and set out to think of a better way than the options that the world makes most obvious. "I went to the woods because I wished to live deliberately, to front only the essential facts of life, and see if I could not learn what it had to teach," wrote Thoreau. "And not, when I came to die, discover that I had not lived."

The other Boss, the Boss from Asbury, New Jersey, wrote in his book, *Songs*, that "Thunder Road" comes down to the ultimate proposition: "Do you want to take a chance? On us? On life?"

Walden and "Thunder Road" may be the same song in different keys. They're about two guys who hit the road, hoping that by creating a little distance between themselves and the way things are, they just might glimpse the way things could be.

Flipping the Math

Thoreau discovered in his twenties what it takes most of us much longer to figure out: The goal of society isn't to help each person thrive. The goal of society is to use the most people in the most productive way to keep the machine running. After his years of work in his father's pencil factory,

Thoreau knew a thing or two about machines. He quickly learned when he was running a machine and when he was a cog in one. He soon discovered that most people are cogs when they think they're machines.

"If you win, society is the loser," Thoreau wrote in his essay, "Life Without Principle." Think of the inverse of that statement: If we lose, society is the winner. While the system pretends to reward rugged individuals determined to achieve success, what it needs most is a mass of unquestioning consumers and workers, endlessly toiling and buying and feeding the machine. Society needs us to be productive; it's up to us to be human.

Thoreau's genius was knowing when it's better to opt out than to be a cog in this machine. He repeatedly urges readers to notice how society uses them—their time, their labor, their money—each day. "Everywhere, in shops, and offices, and fields, the inhabitants have appeared to me to be doing penance in a thousand remarkable ways," he wrote. "It is a fool's life, as they will find when they get to the end of it, if not before." He urges readers to question whether they buy things because they need to have them or because someone needs to sell them.

Some people work to exhaustion because they don't question if another way may exist. Instead, they lock themselves into a cycle: The more they earn, the more they buy, the more they want, and then they need to earn even more to buy that new stuff they now want. And repeat. The alternative, Thoreau reminds us, is to define "enough," to set our ground rules early. What is enough salary? What is enough stuff? What is enough time at work? Once we strive for and achieve enough, we can turn our attention to other things, to life.

Thoreau would've been at home in this moment in American history, as the Great Resignation has given way to the Great Reassessment—the great redefining of "enough." Nearly half of workers considered quitting their jobs in 2024, according to a study by Microsoft and LinkedIn. After the largest trial of a four-day workweek, 15 percent of workers said that "no amount of money" would convince them to go back to five-day workweeks.[1] People realize that they work too much, too hard, for what they get back. Eventually, extra work and additional income bring diminishing returns. We regular folks can do better than this.

While we turn from the old way, however, we don't see a new way to aspire to. That's why we need the 19th-century Boss. Thoreau spent his life persuading people to live lives as humans, not just workers—to be happy, not just useful.

To do this, Thoreau flipped the math. Instead of earning as much as possible and deciding how to spend it, he did the reverse. How little could he earn and still live well? Instead of wondering what he'd need to sacrifice to gain a big house/ nice clothes/cool stuff, he wondered what he could gain by sacrificing the big house/nice clothes/cool stuff.

Thoreau pared life down to mere necessities at Walden Pond—just enough to get by—then worked just long enough to cover them. The guy was a Harvard grad; he could've joined his classmates making fortunes in New York or Boston in law or finance. But he wanted to be a writer in a world that doesn't like to pay writers. (My sympathy may be a side effect of my profession.) His goal was to enjoy work, to enjoy time. He sought to win his own respect, not others' approval. To read *Walden* is to watch Thoreau flip the American Dream upside down.

Before *Walden* becomes an encouraging read, I'll warn you: It can be the stuff of nightmares. The gap between the way things are and the way things could be widens with each turning page. "You suspect, with sudden alarm, that there is more to life than you had been told . . . that Western civilization may have taken the wrong path and may yet have to turn back—or wish desperately that it could," wrote H. M. Tomlinson, an early 20th-century journalist, of the horror of reading *Walden*.[2]

We've lost the narrative on Thoreau. For nearly 175 years, people have dismissed him as an antisocial, contrarian slacker. For the past twenty years or so, people have oddly obsessed over whether he did his own laundry. But now, at last, the world is ready for what Henry David Thoreau can teach us: how to live, and what to live for.

Waldenomics: The Math of the Middle Way

Walden is discussed more than it's read. Because of that, many people get it all wrong. The most common *Walden* myth is that Thoreau was a recluse who claimed to live alone in the wilderness. Not true. In the first sentence of the book, Thoreau tells the reader that his cabin at the pond was "a mile from any neighbour." With this, he reveals that he was a twenty-minute stroll from his friends in Concord—in the first sentence! Then he tells the reader that, as he writes the book, he's left the cabin and he's living in town again—in the third sentence! Reading the first three sentences of this book could clear up many misconceptions about it.

By its reputation, *Walden* seems to be a book about extremes—going minimalist, building a cabin, growing one's own food—but it's really about a search for enough. Thoreau spent just twenty-six months living the minimalist Walden life before he returned to his normal existence in town, working various jobs, supporting his family, becoming a regionally known writer and lecturer. But it was his time at the pond that gave Thoreau the space to learn what he needed back in the real world: enough money, enough stuff, enough success—or rather, just enough.

Buddhists call this the Middle Way. Thoreau, who devoured books on Eastern philosophy, likely knew about the Middle Way. Buddha himself inspired the concept. Siddhartha Guatama—the man who became Buddha—grew up as a prince with tremendous wealth, but he felt unfulfilled by his surroundings. Siddhartha abandoned his title and riches to roam from town to town, hungry and homeless and begging for food, believing he'd discover meaning through deprivation. It turns out that it's harder to attain enlightenment on an empty stomach than with a stuffed belly. Buddha learned to embrace the Middle Way, somewhere between hungry and stuffed, between impoverished and rich. The path to enlightenment can include a decent meal and a comfy bed. That's where Buddha found enough. That's where Thoreau did, too.

Buddha and Thoreau's stories have remarkably similar arcs. They took retreats of scarcity to learn what they really needed and what they did not. Then they returned to the world, finding contentment in enough. "The art of being wise is the art of knowing what to overlook," wrote psychologist William James in *The Principles of Psychology*. To find the Middle Way is to apply this discernment to life.

Embracing the Middle Way can involve a hit to the ego, however, especially in our culture of achievement and accumulation. The Middle Way can be mistaken for the ordinary. And the ordinary can be mistaken for failure.

It's understandable and human that we wish to feel seen, to have our intelligence and hard work recognized and validated. The easiest and most obvious markers of that recognition and validation are material, often appearing as fancy cars, big homes, and nice clothes. The more we collect, the better we're doing, or so it feels. But such a system leads us to focus on how we seem, not how we live.

To embrace the Middle Way is to disentangle our measure of self-worth from our collection of external markers—to focus instead on living well, whatever that means to us. It can be daunting, though. If we don't pursue the highest-paying job and drive the nicest-possible car, will people think we're failing? Will others know that we could have had the impressive title and fancy stuff, if only we had chosen them? Hey, they might. It's a judgy world out there.

Here are better questions: If you live according to your values, with the goal of winning your own respect and enjoying your own time, what would you live for? What wouldn't you care much about? How much do you need to have enough of what matters? Waldenomics is the math we use to discover how much is enough, how much life we're willing to trade for other things. Luckily, there's no right answer. There's only your right answer.

I picture our options on a continuum. Let's call it the continuum of enough. On one end, you'll see a person who lives in an off-the-grid tiny house with a subsistence garden. To them, very little is enough. On the other, you'll see a person with lots of commas in their bank accounts and all the right logos on their stuff who lives to acquire even more. To them, nothing is enough.

We hold those on either end of the continuum as examples of fortitude. We live in a society that wants to crush it, one way or the other. Minimizing life into a tiny house? Crushing it. Climbing that ladder? Crushing it. Choosing a nice-enough home with an enjoyable-enough job that leaves time for hobbies and friends? Well, that carries a whiff of mediocrity. To many, that's not enough.

I can relate. When I hit peak levels of misery at work, my first instinct wasn't to ponder a simpler life or a new career path. Instead, I dreamt of resigning to hike the Appalachian Trail. This may be a reasonable option for some; for me, it's pure insanity. I'm semi-outdoorsy at best. I only camp at drive-in sites that allow me to tote in a large cooler of food and wine, an inflatable mattress, and a stack of books. Camping is merely my excuse to make a campfire-toasted baguette with Brie and a bit of fig jam and catch up on my reading. I'm far from a Thoreau. Yet at work, I had fallen into a paradigm of extremes: I could either strive for a top spot on the organization chart or languish on the Appalachian Trail. Anything between the two seemed like failure, like settling for the ordinary. Since then, I've found joy in the ordinary.

The good news about the continuum of enough lies in the expanse of options between the two extremes. That's where the magic is. Those are the spots where we can create a comfortable lifestyle with what we find essential (electrical grid, Netflix, baguette with Brie and fig jam) while we live our values. To find our spot on that continuum is to find our Walden. It comes when we realize that it is only our opinion of ourselves that matters, not the approval of our neighbors or relatives or bosses. ("What a man thinks of himself, that is which determines, or rather indicates, his fate," Thoreau wrote.) We don't have to live like crows, constantly adding new, shiny things to our nests.

I didn't hike the Appalachian Trail. But I did move from the DC area to the less-expensive Charlotte, North Carolina. After considering impressive MBA programs, I chose a master's program in English at a state school. I eventually quit work as a web developer to become a writer. Let me tell you how unpopular these decisions were, even with well-intentioned people who love me. People worried that I'd compromised my potential, that I'd made an irrevocable break with a promising future. But these decisions gave me more peace and contentment than I've ever had. The car I drive in my forties isn't as nice as the one I drove in my thirties; my home is half the size of many of my friends' houses. My salary is less as a writer of words than it was as a writer of code. But here, in this lovely ordinary life, I've found enough. And it didn't involve my premature death on the Appalachian Trail or suffering in a fluorescent-lit cubicle— nor did it involve the permission or approval of anyone else.

Many people don't have the luxury of choices, however. They're working and simply trying to survive. This book isn't a guide to correcting the economic system that imprisons so many beneath the reach of social mobility. And this book surely doesn't place blame on people who can't find enough in this deeply flawed system. I'm afraid this book would be of little help to a single parent working multiple low-wage jobs and still not finding enough. If I knew that answer, I'd write that book.

This book, like *Walden*, acknowledges the system is rigged and does not have our best interests at heart. And I, like Thoreau, seek to uncover the choices we have in this deeply flawed system, the ones that society doesn't easily reveal—to strategically opt out of the expectations that don't serve us and to invest in the opportunities that do.

To begin, we need to define enough in the two major currencies of Waldenomics: How much stuff is enough? How much time is enough? And how much of either is too much?

Minimalism of Stuff

One of the founders of the 21st-century minimalism movement is Joshua Becker. He didn't set out to spark a movement, however. He just wanted to clean his garage.

On a May afternoon in 2008, Becker and his wife were in the middle of their annual spring garage cleaning when a casual remark from a neighbor sparked an existential crisis. "Ah, the joys of home ownership," the neighbor joked to him. Becker replied, "Well you know what they say— the more stuff you own, the more your stuff owns you."[3]

It could've just become another neighborly exchange of banal pleasantries, forgotten soon after it happened. But after his neighbor went on about her way, Becker stopped cleaning and wondered: Was that true? Did his stuff really own him? At that moment, his five-year-old son was playing alone in the backyard, waiting for his parents to finish organizing the garage. Becker realized that if he and his wife weren't tending to their stuff, they'd all be in the yard playing together. How often did they take care of their stuff instead of being with each other?

That year, Becker launched *BecomingMinimalist.com*, the first website devoted to minimalism, as he began his foray into doing more with less. A two-year process began, in which his family gradually culled 80 percent of their possessions and moved into a smaller home—where they could spend more time with one another, not their stuff. Becker said that reducing how much stuff he owned has positively affected nearly every aspect of his life. Once he questioned the status quo in one area, he began to question it in all others. "It seems like a lot of people are just kind of conforming to culture rather than rather than seeing where culture is leading them down a less intentional path," Becker told me.

Becker's not alone. An increasing number of people wonder, "Do I really need all this stuff? Are my belongings adding to—or subtracting from—my life?" So many people have wanted to learn more about Becker's shift to minimalism that his lifestyle has become his full-time job. More than one million people subscribe to Becker's emails about how to adopt a minimalist lifestyle, and he's published five books on the topic. Minimalism has gone big. Many of us want to learn how to trade up by paring down.

One of the original minimalists was, of course, Thoreau. His cabin at Walden Pond was ten feet by fifteen feet—one door, two windows, a fireplace. Inside, he had a bed, a table, a desk, a lamp, and three chairs. Add in a few utensils and pans, and Thoreau brought a total of twenty-four things to the pond. To build the cabin, he recycled materials from a nearby dissembled shanty, which cost him about $28, or about $1,100 in today's dollars. "My greatest skill has been to want but little," he wrote.

Scarcity was the point. Thoreau wanted to pare down to the absolute basics to learn what added to his life and what subtracted from it. If he could spend the bare minimum on what he truly needed, he could work the bare minimum to afford it. Then he could use the rest of his time doing as he wanted: writing, walking in nature, visiting friends. "When [a person] has obtained those things which are necessary to life, there is another alternative than to obtain the superfluities; and that is, to adventure on life now."

We live in a culture of superfluities. The average American home has 300,000 items in it.[4] We don't just pay for those 300,000 items, we also pay to maintain them, insure them, clean them, update them, power them. We also have bigger homes to fit all this stuff. Through the 1960s, the size of the average home built in the United States was about 1,500 square feet. In the early 2000s, it was about

2,000 square feet. And in 2022, it reached 2,559 square feet.[5] Houses got bigger even as average family sizes got smaller. Those homes aren't just housing people; they're storing our stuff.

About a fifth of households have even more stuff beyond their walls. Twenty-one percent of Americans rent self-storage units, and an additional 15 percent say that they plan to rent one in the future.[6] Not only do we pay for a lot of stuff, but we pay rent for it, too.

Do we really need all this stuff and all this space? Increasingly, people are saying no. American homes are beginning to get smaller; in 2023, the size of the average single-family home went down to 2,200 square feet, according to the National Association of Homebuilders—the lowest it's been in more than a decade. All this stuff and square footage cost too much, in the Waldenomics sense.

MODERN-DAY THOREAUS

About 165 years after Thoreau moved into his cabin, Ryan Nicodemus packed everything he owned in his 2,000-square-foot condo into moving boxes. Here's the weird thing: Nicodemus wasn't moving.

Inspired by the minimalism of his best friend Joshua Fields Millburn, Nicodemus wanted to learn how many possessions he really needed. Nicodemus went total Thoreau.

He packed everything into labeled boxes and removed items only as he needed them: a laptop, a spatula, a jacket. Three weeks later, 80 percent of his stuff was still packed. He donated or sold everything left in a box. In his essay, "Packing Party: Unpack a Simpler Life," he wrote, "I started to feel rich for the first time in my life. I felt rich once I got everything out of the way, so I could make room for everything that remains." Or, as Thoreau wrote, "A man is rich in proportion to the number of things which he can afford to let alone."

The results of Nicodemus's experiment created a cascading effect. If Nicodemus didn't need that much stuff, he didn't need that much condo. Without that much mortgage, he didn't need the corporate job he hated. He quit. His luxury car soon seemed superfluous. He sold it. Nicodemus realized, just as Becker did, that his stuff had owned him. He didn't miss the stuff, but he loved his new freedom. He and Fields Millburn moved to Montana and lived in a cabin as writers for several years, calling it "an updated version of the whole Thoreau thing."[7]

If you think they went extreme, consider the other extreme minimalists of the early 21st century. A guy named Dave Bruno culled his possessions to just one hundred items, which inspired his book, *The 100 Thing Challenge*. And then there was Niels Borhmann, who reduced his possessions to only those that would fit into a backpack—about fifteen items—even sacrificing furniture and opting to sleep on the floor. Borhmann out-Thoreau'ed even Thoreau himself.

Nicodemus and Fields Millburn went on to become The Minimalists, darlings of the early 2000s minimalist movement. More than a decade later, The Minimalists still preach the less-stuff, more-freedom gospel, with a documentary, books, and podcast attesting to the demand of their ever-growing congregation.

FINDING THE MIDDLE WAY OF MINIMALISM

Becker, whom many credit with popularizing the term "minimalism" when he launched his website, didn't intend for the movement to go extreme. He encourages people to simply be more intentional, to find their Middle Way of minimalism. "This isn't about how many numbers of things you own," he told me. "It's about owning what you need to own to live your best life, and that's always going to look different for each person."

This will also look different for each person at each stage of life. Becker said that, for him, being a minimalist with a five-year-old son looked far different from being a minimalist with two teenage kids. It'll look different for a single person in the city versus a big family on a farm. And that's okay. For most people, minimalism is a movement that tosses stuff that doesn't spark joy (thank you, Marie Kondo), that politely declines family heirlooms (sorry, Grandma), and that would rather enjoy an evening with friends than buy a new shirt (you're welcome, craft breweries). It's a movement that second guesses what we need and what we're better off without. As Thoreau wrote, "Most of the luxuries, and many of the so-called comforts of life, are not only not indispensable, but positive hindrances to the elevation of mankind."

I'd argue that overflowing closets and stuffed drawers are also hindrances to the elevation of mankind, or at least hindrances to a good day. Nothing spikes the blood pressure quite like sorting through piles of things we don't like to try to find that one thing we do or shoving stuff down into a drawer to make it close. When deciding whether to buy a new item—a sweater, a vase, some shoes—it helps to think of it not as a one-time purchase but as the start of a new relationship. Am I willing to find a place for this thing in my home for the next few years, or am I better off keeping the space and time that it would consume?

For many, minimalism isn't about sacrifice but peace. Melissa Russell of Alberta, Canada, came to minimalism after the death of her first child when he was just nineteen days old. Grief clarified her priorities, and she wanted to clear room for what mattered most. She started getting rid of the stuff she "thought she loved," mostly stuff bought because it was on sale but then rarely used. Then she de-cluttered any décor that didn't hold special meaning to her family but just added to the things they had to clean. She reduced the items in her home by at least half over the next few years. Today, Russell is a mom to three children, and she runs the Simple Lionheart Life blog devoted to minimalism (named in honor of her first child, Aiden, whom she nicknamed "Aiden the Lionheart"). I asked Russell what it's like to be both a minimalist and a parent, and she said that minimalism allows her to be the parent she wants to be. "Having less stuff in our home means I spend less time managing and taking care of it all," she wrote to me. "Instead, I have more time for things I love most. I have more time to spend with my family. I have more time to explore hobbies I love like painting, reading, and yoga. I feel less rushed and overwhelmed, like I can easily manage our home and our lives without it being too much."

The minimalism movement has gone mainstream. "Simple-sizing" is the term Opendoor uses to describe the trend of people thinking of less as more. Their recent survey of adults of all ages showed that 79 percent of respondents intended to downsize possessions within the year. When polled about their dream home, nearly two-thirds of respondents said that their idea of a dream home had shifted over the last three years to something smaller and simpler. That single-family home is likely to just get smaller from here.

Just as Thoreau returned from Walden Pond to live in his family home and find his spot within the Middle Way, surrounded by his books and plant samples and tools, The Minimalists didn't stay in that cabin in Montana. Their extreme minimalism evolved as they each got married, bought their own homes, started new stages of life. They began to accumulate again, but this time deliberately, to discover their Middle Way. Theirs aren't lifestyles dictated by rules and absolutes, but by intentionality. Fields Millburn wrote, "Over time, though, situations'll change—they always do. So I'm forced to ask the same important question over and over and over again: *Does this thing add value to my life?* In other words: does it serve a purpose or bring me joy?"[8]

Minimalism of Time

Picture a meditation session, and you'll likely picture someone at home sitting serenely, cross-legged, with their eyes gently closed. What I'm about to mention isn't that kind of meditation session. This is corpse meditation, a centuries-old tradition during which Buddhist monks meditate in the presence of decomposing bodies. The idea is to remind oneself that, with 100 percent certainty, we will look a lot like that rotting body one day. (The mantra during corpse meditation: "This body of mine, too, is of the same nature as that body, is going to be like that body.")

It's intense, sure, but we can't argue with the point. The idea of corpse meditation is to fully dwell in the present moment when our bodies can walk around, when our minds can ponder, when we can still . . . do stuff. It's a stark reminder that at any moment, we can go from this—the walking, the pondering, the doing stuff—to becoming "like that body." Corpse meditation is a stark (and pungent) reminder that time, more than money, is our most valuable currency.

Thoreau understood this all too well. He caught tuberculosis when he was about eighteen, during the TB pandemic that swept North America and Europe during the 19th century. Then, not many people with the disease saw the other side of forty. Thoreau's grandfather died of the disease; his sister, Helen, did, too. His father died after suffering from symptoms of TB. Thoreau knew his life wouldn't be long, but he insisted it would be interesting.

A pandemic changed our view of time, too, especially during the spring of 2020 when we didn't understand how COVID passed or whom it would harm. Everyone became vulnerable. Think of how we spent our time during those early, scary months. We'd drive to someone's home just to wave at them from the driveway; we'd bang pots and pans to thank health care workers; we'd take walks with neighbors and host happy hours on Zoom. With everything on the line, we prioritized what was priceless: our time to connect.

Just as the early 2000s saw a rise in the minimalism of stuff, a new movement began in the 2020s: a minimalism of time. It applies Waldenomics to our schedule: Which uses of our time pay us back? And which cost us more than they give us?

SPENDING OUR FOUR THOUSAND WEEKS WELL

Corpse meditation may seem a bit much to consider, so let's downshift to something less visual and more numeric: Oliver Burkeman's book, *Four Thousand Weeks: Time Management for Mortals*. Four thousand weeks—that's about how much time most of us have on this earth. It doesn't sound nearly enough, does it? Surely, the average person has more than four thousand Saturday nights? More than four thousand Taco Tuesdays? Add those weeks up, however, and you get 76.7 years. What will we do with our wild and precious four thousand weeks, to paraphrase Mary Oliver?

Burkeman writes that accepting this limited time means advocating fiercely for how we spend each minute—and, equally importantly, how we shouldn't. "The more firmly you believe it ought to be possible to find time for everything, the less pressure you'll feel to ask whether any given activity is the best use for a portion of your time," he wrote. "If you never stop to ask yourself if the sacrifice is worth it, your days will automatically begin to fill not just with more things, but with more trivial or tedious things, because they've never had to clear the hurdle of being judged more important than something else."

Time is a zero-sum game, so spending more of it well requires spending less of it poorly. For many of us, the two primary culprits that hijack time well spent are unnecessary hours with our phones and our jobs. Think about the percent of your waking hours that you don't spend either scrolling or working—likely very few. Now think how many times you wished you spent *more* time scrolling or working—likely never. The time minimalist movement helps us align our time with our values.

We can't ditch our phones or our jobs, alas. But we can reevaluate how much time we spend with them, turning into fierce advocates for how we spend our most valuable currency.

DEFINING ENOUGH: TIME WITH OUR PHONES

Tiffany Shlain may seem an unexpected person to convince people to ditch their phones. She founded the Webby

Awards, an annual celebration of the best of the internet; she owes her professional life to technology. But on Friday evenings, she turns off her phone for twenty-four hours in a digital Sabbath, a habit that the digital professional suggests that other over-connected people should adopt. "This can be adapted for anyone, wherever you fall on the belief spectrum," Shlain said in an interview with *Word&Way*. "And it will bring meaning and value to your life in unbelievable ways."[9]

Americans spend an average of four hours and twenty-five minutes on their phone each day (each day!), not including time spent on phone calls. That means we spend more than two months of our year scrolling. More than half of Americans say that they feel addicted to their phone.[10] It's not surprising: The same tricks that keep people mindlessly pulling the handle of a slot machine are the ones that keep us mindlessly clicking, well past the point we know it's good for us.

I find it telling that the idea of the Sabbath has found a secular reimagining in technological terms: the digital Sabbath, the social media Sabbath. The idea of reserving time away from our phones seems nothing short of religious. We can find the divine when we lose our phones.

Rabbi Abraham Joshua Heschel called the Sabbath "a cathedral in time," a beautiful reminder that time itself, when used well, can create sacred space. Yet it's difficult to put our phones away, considering the notifications that knock down our cathedrals in time, brick by brick, click by click. We say that we pay too much attention to our phones, but that's not quite accurate. We pay for our phones *with* too much of our attention. Political scientist Herbert Simon wrote, "In an information-rich world, the wealth of information means a dearth of something else: a scarcity of whatever it is that information consumes. What information consumes is rather obvious: it consumes the attention of its recipients. Hence a wealth of information creates a poverty of attention."[11]

Simon wrote that in 1971, the year that introduced the personal computer. Imagine what he'd write today if he had lived long enough to know that we walk around with much more powerful computers in our pockets, spending four and a half hours each day looking at them. If the cost of a thing is the amount of life we trade for it, imagine what our phones truly cost us.

This is why more of us, like Shlain, build guardrails around our phones. We want some of that life back. In *Digital Minimalism*, Cal Newport suggests that people adopt a "philosophy of technology use" that creates rules around when and why we use our devices—and when and why we shouldn't. He encourages people to become digital minimalists. Digital minimalists "don't mind missing out on the small things; what worries them much more is diminishing the large things they already know for sure make life good."[12]

My philosophy of technology use is the digital moat strategy. For one hour before work and one hour after work, I carve out a moat of screen-free time. No phone, no laptop, no just checking in on email. Before work, I read a book and enjoy quiet. After work, I play with my dogs, cook dinner with my husband, and poke around in my garden. It forces me to contain work within the confines of working hours, without it crossing the moat into my real life. It's also a twice-daily reminder of how much better my brain feels when I take a break from notifications and screens to focus on real things and actual people. Others limit screen time by opting for old-school phones, even temporarily (such as Flip Phone February). Even new phones can come with a strange selling point: fewer features. Two former app developers for Google, Joe Hollier and Kaiwei Tong, invented the Light Phone, which offers limited app options beyond basics like an alarm clock and text messaging. "It's a way to enjoy quality time away from the pressures of the smartphone," according to the phone's site. It's a curious selling point that reveals something about our cultural moment: Buy this phone so you'll use it less.

Then, of course, we can use our phone itself as an ally to help us build our cathedrals in time. One of the most amusing phone guardrails I've seen is The Forest app. When you download the app, you can "plant" a seed and watch it grow into a beautiful tree on your screen. The moment you check social media, however, you kill your tree—"as if you could kill time without injuring eternity," Thoreau wrote, or perhaps without killing your digital tree.

DEFINING ENOUGH: TIME AT WORK

In 2022, a man named Zaid Khan proposed a radical idea: What if he spent more time going above and beyond in his personal life and less time doing so at work? What would it look like to prioritize being a human over being a worker? He laid out his strategy on TikTok: "You're not outright quitting your job, but you're quitting the idea of going above and beyond. You're still performing your duties, but you're no longer subscribing to the hustle culture mentality that work has to be your life. The reality is, it's not, and your worth as a person is not defined by your labor."

America lost its mind. In the United States, this isn't sticking to a job description; this is quiet quitting. "If you're a quiet quitter, you're a loser,"[13] said Kevin O'Leary from *Shark Tank*. "When you bring somebody in that slams shut their laptop at 5:00, you're introducing a cancer into your culture."[13] Arianna Huffington called quiet quitting "a step toward quitting on life."[14]

If leaving work on time introduces a cancer into American culture, workers aren't the ones who are sick; this culture is. The problem of the 21st century isn't that American workers don't work enough. This isn't about what we choose to do for work (we'll dive into that in a later chapter) but how much time we are willing to spend doing it. And, increasingly, workers demand a halt to hustle culture.

Workdays have become amorphous things. An Asana survey revealed that 37 percent of workers have workdays without clearly defined start and end times. Even worse, people estimate that they spend more than half of their working hours doing "work about work." This includes emailing about meetings and asking for status reports.[15]

Previously, companies tried to make long workdays attractive through perks like on-site gyms, free snacks, and nap rooms. Now, those perks look like shackles. Increasingly, workers demand something more valuable than an office golf simulator. They want some of their time back.

Recent years have introduced a new bit of math into Waldenomics: how much a commute costs our time, our energy, and our bottom line. Half of people who work from home said they'd look for a new job if their current job forced them into an office. Research showed that people valued the option to work remotely as much as they would an 8 percent raise.[16] These hypotheticals have gained real-life case studies. In 2024, Dell Technologies gave its remote workers an ultimatum: Either return to the office or become ineligible for promotions. Nearly half of those workers still stayed home, preferring a home office to a raise. Workers demand to be evaluated by their output, not their hours or location; after all, hard work can happen at home, and slacking can happen in an office. "Before quiet quitting, there was Microsoft Solitaire," said Stephen Meier, the chair of Columbia Business School Management Division, in an article in *Fortune*.[17]

Four-day workweeks also bring positive results to both employees and employers. During the 2023 annual meeting of the World Economic Forum, one presenter called the four-day workweek "a business imperative." This followed research done in the United States, Ireland, Australia, and New Zealand that showed the shorter work week made people healthier, happier, and more productive. (It helped the environment, too. Fewer commutes mean fewer CO_2 emissions.)

Remote work and four-day workweeks are not about "a step toward quitting on life." They're about working smarter, about containing work within reasonable hours so that workers can work to live and not live to work.

American workers saved sixty million hours by not com-
muting during the pandemic—and they were healthier for
it. Data from the American Time Use Survey showed that
these workers slept, on average, an extra hour a night. They
enjoyed leisure activities for about two more hours a day.
In other words, they traded time as workers to enjoy time
as well-rounded, healthy humans. People realized that they
could make better use of their 4,000 weeks. They, like Thoreau, learned to expect more from their time.

"I go forth to make new demands on life," Thoreau journaled at age thirty-four, when he had just 531 weeks left.

Five Questions:
The Math of Waldenomics

1. If you redefine currency as Thoreau does—that the
   cost of things is the amount of life that we trade
   for them—which items in your life seem too ex-
   pensive to buy, and which seem too valuable to
   sacrifice?

2. In the same Waldenomics way of thinking, what is
   one way you spend your time that brings you an
   outsized profit?

3. How much of your possessions would you be
   willing to part with or to downsize to gain more

freedom, space, money, or time? Consider it all—
home, car, clothes, devices, furniture.

4. If you had to begin decluttering your stuff today,
   where would you begin and how would it affect
   your life?

5. Now, the same question for your schedule: If you
   had to begin decluttering your time today, where
   would you begin and how would it affect your life?

Create Space between You and the World

Find peace—and insight— with a little distance.

I love to be alone. I never found the companion that was so companionable as solitude.
—HENRY DAVID THOREAU

Here lies the paradox of solitude. Look long and hard enough at yourself in isolation and suddenly you will see the rest of humanity staring back.
—STEPHEN BATCHELOR

W hat compelled a Harvard-educated writer to walk
into the woods, build a cabin, live alone, and plant
beans? These are hardly the actions of someone whose life
has gone to plan. Let's roll back the tape a couple years.

On December 3, 1843, about eighteen months before
Thoreau embarked on his Walden Pond retreat, he returned
from a lesser-known experiment. Thoreau lived in New
York City to jump-start his writing career. He moved to
Staten Island, where he earned room and board and a small
stipend for tutoring three sons of a wealthy family. Thoreau
had a solid plan: When he wasn't tutoring, he'd commute
into Manhattan, meet with editors, and become a famous
writer. Seems solid, right?

Thoreau wasn't the first to have a dream crushed by
the big city. He didn't get on well with the family, so he
felt lonely for his circle of friends back in Concord. Plus,
the literary scene was tougher than he expected. While
the city offered more opportunities for writers, it also had
more writers competing for editors' attention. "My bait will
not tempt the rats—they are too well fed," Thoreau wrote
to his mother that fall. The writing opportunities that the
rats—er, editors—offered usually paid too little to even
make a living. And in true New York fashion, the commute
was miserable. It took half a day for Thoreau to get into
Manhattan from Staten Island; the trip involved a boat ride

and several miles of walking (he couldn't afford the bus)—a long way to travel for disappointment.

Thoreau scored a few bylines, but instead of making money writing for magazines, he was forced to make money by selling them. Thoreau, a mega-introvert not interested in small talk or business, got by in New York City by selling subscriptions to *American Agriculturalist* magazine door-to-door. It was hardly his big-city dream. New York City's cultural offerings hardly won him over either. An entry in his journal shows him un-wowed by city life: "I hate museums; there is nothing so weighs upon my spirits. They are the catacombs of nature. . . . The life that is in a single green weed is of more worth than all this death. They are dead nature collected by dead men." This is not a happy man. Thoreau's New York experiment lasted six months.

When he returned to Concord, Thoreau didn't escape financial pressures. His parents were preparing to buy their first house, one that his mother would run as a boarding home to earn additional income. After the death of his older brother John, Thoreau dutifully fulfilled the duties of eldest son, and he contributed money toward his parents' $500 down payment (quite possibly using the earnings from his door-to-door salesman work). He even dug the cellar of their home and lined its walls with stones, helped the carpenter with repairs, and planted an orchard on the property.

If the price of a thing is the amount of life we trade for it, his parents' house cost Thoreau quite a lot in the Walde-nomics sense. Around this time, his father's pencil business began to falter, so Thoreau further interrupted his writing career to lend his dad a hand in the factory.

By then, Thoreau was twenty-eight, and he'd done all the responsible things. He got a top-tier education. He went to the city to make it big. He helped his parents buy a home and supported the family business. But he couldn't do what he wanted to do most: Enjoy a simple life as a work-ing writer. His close friend Ellery Channing wrote to him in early 1845, noting Thoreau's frustration: "I see nothing for you in this earth but that field which I once christened 'Briars'; go out upon that, build yourself a hut, & there begin the grand process of devouring yourself alive."

Four months after he received that letter, Thoreau was in the woods near an old briar patch by Walden Pond, building a cabin. This experiment would be the exact op-posite of his New York City one.

Walden Pond was not a vacation. Walden Pond was a retreat, full of intention and purpose. There, Thoreau min-imized his expenses and distractions to focus on grander ideas. He still worked, a lot: He wrote freelance articles and gave lectures at the town lyceum (the TED Talks of his day); he made money as the town handyman. He wrote the book that he believed would be his life's work, *A Week on the Concord and Merrimack Rivers.* (The book would flop. The topic of his true masterpiece, meanwhile, was literally under his nose as he wrote it.)

In Tibet, this kind of life experiment is called "adding wood to the fire." It's an expression that describes a voluntary act of temporarily making life more difficult so as to access a deeper truth. Think of people who train for a marathon; they train to run 26.2 miles, sure, but they most likely seek to attain something greater than mileage. "Adding wood to the fire" allows us to challenge ourselves to confront difficulty and reveal what's been within us all along.

"When we are not constricted by habitual patterns that define how we see ourselves and how we behave in the world, we create access to those qualities of mind that are vast, that are not contingent on circumstances or concepts . . . the very essence of our true nature," wrote Yongey Mingyur Rinpoche in *In Love with the World: A Monk's Journey through the Bardos of Living and Dying.* The monk had gone on a wandering retreat—alone, without food, and at times dangerously close to death—to explore who he really was and what he really needed.

Thoreau's cabin seems like a five-star hotel in comparison to Mingyur Rinpoche's retreat, but the two men's goals were the same: to leave the comforts and routine of everyday life to access what lies within. Two days after he moved into his cabin, Thoreau journaled these words, precursors to *Walden*'s most famous passage: "I wish to meet the facts of life—the vital facts, which are the phenomena or actuality the gods meant to show us—face to face, and so I came down here. Life! who knows what it is, what it does? If I am not quite right here, I am less wrong than before."

Thoreau moved into his cabin on July 4, 1845. He claims it was just "by accident" that he chose Independence Day to begin his retreat. I don't believe him.

Going Away to Return to Ourselves

Thoreau joined a long line of people who retreat from the world to gain clarity upon their return to it. Think Jesus, Buddha, Moses—Luke Skywalker, even. The goal of a retreat isn't to go away forever; it's to come home different.

Even though Thoreau sought space at Walden Pond, he stumbled into an unexpected bit of celebrity there. Word spread of his experiment, and people had a lot to say about a man who opted against a full-time job—much of it not good. In a letter to the editor in the *New York Tribune*, one man wrote about Thoreau's retreat to Walden: "The young man is either a whimsy or else a good-for-nothing, selfish, crab-like sort of chap, who tries to shirk the duties. . . .

Such a way of going on . . . is both infernal and infernally stupid."[1]

In a culture in which productivity defines self-worth, retreats can be a hard sell. That was true then and is true now. That hasn't always been the case, however.

For most of humanity, retreats weren't about shirking duties. They were about being human. When it was time to think the big thoughts of life—to beg forgiveness, to seek miracles, to discover purpose—religions and cultures told people to get the heck out of town. Epiphanies and reflections belonged in shrines, at altars, atop mountains. Ancient Greeks traveled to temples to seek divine intervention. Buddhists and Hindus have traveled to Bodh Gaya in India since the 3rd century BCE to contemplate and ask for blessings. Since the 7th century, Muslims have made annual pilgrimages to Mecca to cleanse their souls and proclaim good intentions. Catholics have walked Spain's 500-mile Camino de Santiago in Spain for spiritual retreat since the 9th century. While many of these traditions continue, they're practiced by a dwindling group of seekers. Today, we must cram in a quest for enlightenment sometime between doing the dishes and brushing our teeth before bed.

I don't mean to romanticize the days of the ancient Greeks, which were hardly halcyon years for the slaves who built many of those temples and shrines. I do believe, though, sacrificing shared cultural traditions (which focus on the big picture of life) for capitalist values (which focus on quarterly earnings) has cost us something vitally human. We've lost the art of retreat—basically, taking a grown-up time-out to think about what it is we're doing, exactly. Instead, we're like toddlers, exhausted and moody yet insistent we don't need a nap.

The *New York Times* writer Ezra Klein said during his podcast that he felt that the sands of his hourglass were slipping endlessly into Google Calendar blocks. I've never looked at my Google Calendar the same. What does this cost us—and what does this cost our culture at large— to live in a society that devours our lives thirty minutes at a time but doesn't encourage us to reserve moments for contemplation? At what point will we stop getting smarter and just get busier? Or have we already?

Philosopher Alain de Botton believes that trading the millennia-old tradition of retreat for the lure of immediacy has had very real costs to our mental health—as well as to the progress of humanity itself. When we focus on the immediate, we lose sight of the important. "The deep, immersive thinking which produced many of civilization's most important achievements has come under unprecedented assault," he wrote in *Religion for Atheists: A Non-Believer's Guide to the Uses of Religion.* Instead of looking far ahead of us, we look just inches from our noses and wonder why we don't have peace. "The feelings and thoughts which we have omitted to experience while looking at our screens are left to find their revenge in involuntary twitches and our ever-decreasing ability to fall asleep when we should."

Humans weren't meant to endure the day-to-day grind without time and space to reflect. Yet here we are, in a culture in which almost half of American workers don't take all their paid vacation time. And those vacation allowances, usually between eleven and fifteen days a year, hardly provide an ambitious target to hit. When Americans do take vacation time, more than half of them admit they spend part of it working.[2] While corporations prioritize annual retreats to align day-to-day work with long-term mission, too many of them aren't as generous in encouraging their employees to do the same with their personal lives.

Much like Thoreau's lifetime, any break we take usually originates from our own initiative and may be met with disapproval—sometimes from our bosses, sometimes from ourselves—that we're not working hard enough, that we can't hack the grind. (Who wants to be called a "crab-like sort of chap"?) I once worked with a man who bragged about not taking a single vacation day or sick day for four years in a row, even after the births of his children. Um, congrats?

Think of the irony: Thoreau, a writer who worked so hard to break into New York City publications, largely failed at it. But when he decided to do his own thing, he made the pages of the *New York Tribune* as a maligned subject of an editorial. It's more respectable to be a failure in the city than a happy man in the woods, it seems. Still, Thoreau insisted on taking a retreat to seek a kind of divine intervention. He wasn't a religious guy, so he had no sacred place of pilgrimage. He found one: Walden Pond. He knew that he had to create space from the world to follow the wanderings of his mind.

So do we. When we take a moment to separate from the world, we begin to discover our own thoughts, regain our interiority. Who are we, really? What do we think about when our minds have space to wander? What do we value? And what seems less important?

To create space between ourselves and everyone else is to create the mental space to distinguish our goals from our values. Dr. Pooja Lakshmin, in *Real Self Care*, explains the difference. Goals are the objectives we have, the things we hope to accomplish. Values are the qualities we aspire to embody each day, whether we achieve our goals. In other words, goals are what we do, values are who we are. Without a break from our daily grind, it's easy to focus on our goals and neglect our values—even though values have a greater effect on the quality of our lives and our sense of purpose. And if we set our goals without knowing our values, our lives become nothing more than disjointed to-do lists. The sands of our hourglass endlessly slip into Google Calendar blocks.

de Botton imagines the hypothetical role of a "psychoanalytically astute travel agent" who would help us create escapes to the shrines or meccas that would offer the healing powers we need at a particular time for a particular need. Such a travel agent could advise us what to do once we got there—which paintings to see, which books to read, which people to talk with, which paths to walk—to wrest meaning and healing from a place, to reconnect us to our values.

This is exactly what Thoreau did at Walden Pond. Walden Pond was his shrine, his temple. He was his own psychoanalytically astute travel agent.

A two-year, two-month retreat like Thoreau's isn't possible for most of us. If only. There are bills, kids, pets, and, of course, jobs. A growing number of people, however, fight to incorporate retreat into their lives. In summer 2023, more working Americans took vacation days than they had in 2019.[3] More Americans than ever take career breaks. There's nothing like a societal shutdown to teach the lesson of life beyond work.

For many, like Thoreau, this time off is more than vacation. It's an intentional, focused time devoted to self-discovery. Studies show that people return from retreats feeling centered, happier, and healthier. A purposeful retreat—even for minutes a day—can physically change the body and brain, creating a health and wellness boost that lasts long after the retreat ends. There are many ways to accomplish this, but there are three essential aspects of a retreat:

1. To search for greater understanding of identity, purpose, or long-term needs
2. To give the mind space and time to wander
3. To spend time away from routine, either alone or with like-minded retreaters

A retreat isn't about splurging; it's about being human. We need our own Ellery Channing to tell us to go, to begin the grand process of devouring ourselves alive. But there are far louder voices telling us to hit the next deadline, check the next to-do, climb the next rung. It's up to us, then, to hit pause, create a little space, and listen to the voice that too often gets shouted over: our own.

Meditation, the Microdosing of Retreats

Here's a secret of retreat, courtesy of Thoreau: We don't have to go far to get away. Before his Walden experiment, Thoreau turned down a friend's offer to join him for a European adventure. His friend wrote, "Let us take a walk over the fairest portion of the planet Earth and make it ours. . . . The wide world is before us beckoning us to come let us accept and embrace it." An irresistible opportunity, right? Not for Thoreau. In *Walden*, he mentioned the closer destination he wished to travel: "Direct your eye right inward, and you'll find / A thousand regions in your mind / Yet undiscovered. Travel them."

Thoreau built his cabin just a mile and a half from town. It was far enough for where he wanted to go: inside his own head.

A retreat can be about time more than place. Today, we don't have to go anywhere to get away. We can create our own little cathedral of time, just ten or twenty minutes at a shot, right where we are. Enter meditation, the microdosing of retreat.

Meditation, which requires zero equipment and can be done anywhere for free, has become a $6.6 billion international industry.[4] Apps, classes, studios, and retreat centers have brought this 5,000-year-old practice into the 21st century with an ambitious goal: to teach us to turn off devices, sit still, and be present in this moment. The amount of money we spend to help us meditate is proof: We struggle with this—a lot. It seems nothing short of countercultural to sit still and allow our minds to just be.

Why does meditation—in which we seemingly do nothing and go nowhere—count as a retreat? Because meditation is a focused use of time that creates space from the world to give us a piece of ourselves back. Ask anyone who meditates, and they'll tell you how it's changed them. Consult studies, and data will back them up. So will I.

Insomnia led me to try meditation a decade ago. I didn't know how to turn my mind off, and with that, I forgot how to sleep. When I first attempted to meditate, it went like this: I settled into a comfortable, cross-legged position, gently closed my eyes, then proceeded to berate myself for ten minutes for my failure to silence my mind. Not exactly the picture of serenity. Classes in vipassana meditation showed me a better way: I learned to visualize thoughts as clouds that appear and then pass, allowing blue skies to return. I learned not to buy into every thought as truth. This is what people refer to when they mention mindfulness meditation, and it sounds lovely, yes? Not at first. For weeks, my meditations were so restless that I wished my cushion had a seatbelt to keep me still. So many clouds, so little sky.

With time, meditation became easier. I eventually went on a four-day silent meditation retreat that allowed me to rest in the present moment as easily as floating in a pool. Soon, the effects began to creep into my day-to-day life. I worry and judge a bit less; I notice a bit more. And hey, I sleep better, too.

This is more than a shift in perception. This results from physical changes to the brain. When this happens—when meditation changes a person beyond the meditation period—they're called altered traits, which is also the name of the landmark book on mediation by researchers Daniel Goleman and Richard J. Davidson. (Compare this to "altered states," which are the cognitive changes that occur during only the meditation period itself.) The two psychologists have done decades of research using electroencephalogram (EEG) and functional magnetic resonance imaging (fMRI) to measure changes to the brain in novice and long-term meditators. Scans show changes to the brain in long-term meditators, proving it's a form of cardio for the mind. It's an exercise that builds muscle—the most important muscle. It trains the amygdala, the part of the brain ready to spot danger and freak out, to calm the heck down.

It nudges the prefrontal circuitry, the executive functions of learning, deciding, and long-term planning, to kick it up a notch. This allows us to acknowledge thoughts without a knee-jerk response. In a culture that's determined to hijack our attention through outrage, this altered trait holds great power. And how do we gain this superpower? We learn to do nothing, and we practice doing nothing until we can do it well.

Nicole Donnelly runs a marketing firm in Ashburn, Virginia. Every day, she steps away from a schedule stacked with client and staff meetings, goes outside her home office, lies in a hammock, breathes deeply, hugs her body, and dwells in the present moment. Even during the busiest of days, she prioritizes these moments of quiet. How long she does this depends on what her body and mind need that day. Sometimes she lies in that hammock for five minutes, sometimes an hour. At first, her hammock sessions were more stressful than restful: *Was her mindfulness productive enough? Should she be journaling about it?* Results, she found, only came when she stopped trying so hard and learned to accept the present moment as enough. Donnelly said that adding this little bit of nothing to her day has changed her life beyond the meditation period.

"The thing I've noticed the most is incredible self-awareness," she said. "It helps me assess. What do I need to change? Why am I feeling this way? It helps me get to the root of why I am feeling angry or sad so I can figure out what I need."

Another form of meditation is compassion meditation, sometimes known as loving-kindness meditation, or metta. During compassion meditation, a meditator focuses on feelings of good will toward the self and others, even toward people they don't like. Research shows it just takes seven hours of compassion meditation over two weeks until the circuits in the brain responsible for empathy and positivity increase connectivity. In just fourteen days, we can meditate our way to become nicer people. Or, perhaps, we can meditate our way to return to the nice people we've been all along: "The fact that [these results] appear outside the formal meditation state itself may reflect our innate wiring for basic goodness," Goleman and Davidson wrote in *Altered Traits*.

As a transcendentalist, Thoreau believed that people are, by nature, good. And the more that we create a little space between ourselves and the world, the more we can access what's been within us all along. Meditation creates just enough space.

The overlap between Thoreau and meditation is not coincidence. While he was at Walden Pond, he began reading the Bhagavad Gita—an ancient Hindu text that tells of a higher nature within each person—which became a sacred text to him. Thoreau didn't have access to studies using fMRI to tell him that spending time in the present moment helped the brain, but his life was evidence enough that it did. "In any weather, at any hour of the day or night, I have been anxious to improve the nick of time, and notch it on my stick too; to stand on the meeting of two eternities, the past and future, which is precisely the present moment; to toe that line." What is meditation but toeing that line between the past and the future?

By clearing distractions and removing sensory inputs, we can alter the physical structure and workings of the brain, helping us become more relaxed, more focused, and even nicer. When done regularly, this simplest of retreats can connect us to the higher nature within.

We can change the physical structure of our brains by how we focus our attention for minutes at a time. I have a hard time deciding which is more shocking: what happens to our minds when we take a moment to dwell in the present or what happens to our minds if we don't.

Intentional Travel as Retreat

When Alain de Botton imagined the role of a psychoanalytically astute travel agent, he was close to imagining Dr. Alisha Reed. She's a licensed pharmacist in New Orleans who believes that retreat can be a form of medicine. In addition to her career in medicine, Dr. Reed began a business in which she prescribes retreats for clients: They come to her with their stressors and needs, and she helps them design a getaway that will serve them long after they return.

For some clients, Dr. Reed may prescribe a weekend of meditation and yoga in a luxury spa in a faraway city. For others, she'll suggest booking a local hotel room and using a staycation to reconnect with a hobby, perhaps picking up an old writing project, taking a class, or simply enjoying solitude. "I ask clients to define what it is that they need from this time, what they seek," Dr. Reed said. "Then I help them curate activities and stress the importance of self-care."

The idea of retreats as a form of medicine came to Dr. Reed in 2019, after her forty-three-year-old husband died from a heart attack. He was a successful attorney who worked long hours in a high-stress job. Dr. Reed learned that taking breaks wasn't a splurge; it was vital to being human. She told me that she gave up her quest to be a supermom who never took a break. Now she uses retreat as a form of preventive medicine, and she's become a calmer mom and happier person.

"A lot of people don't realize that when you do see a doctor, sometimes they'll tell you that rest is best," she told me. "Aside from medication, I definitely do think that it's an option to take breaks and reevaluate things. Retreat gives you that opportunity."

THE SCIENCE OF RETREAT

What if I told you that you could justify a vacation as a Thoreauvian retreat? You can (and you're welcome). The line between vacay and retreat doesn't depend on where you go or how long you stay there—although those are factors, and we'll get to those in a minute—but it depends on the mindset you bring to the trip. Done intentionally, going away for a few days to appreciate the taste of another life can help you appreciate your own life more upon your return.

Travel is an art. Anyone who's planned a trip knows that. But thanks to Michael Brein, travel is a science, too.

Brein was the first person to coin the term "travel psychology." While he worked on his PhD in social psychology in Hawaii, he also spent time with the Peace Corps in Tonga and took language classes in Chinese and Indonesian. He's traveled to more than 125 countries. Through it all, he realized that being in different places and interacting with different cultures can change a person long after the trip ends. What is it about a temporary change of address that turns us into different people? Why does seeing more of the world teach us more about ourselves?

"The more that you travel, the more you morph from a tourist to a traveler to an adventurer to an explorer," said

Brein, who now lives on Bainbridge Island, Washington. "The more you connect with people and places and things overseas, you gain positive interactions. You cannot help but bring some of this back."

Over the past fifty years, Brein has interviewed nearly two thousand people about their travel stories. Where did they go? What did they learn? How did it change them? These stories became data. Retreat has become the stuff of research, leaping from Brein's desk to become its own field. Here's what researchers have learned so far.

Retreat Lesson 1: How You Travel Is More Important Than Where You Travel

A 2012 Dutch study on the effects of travel on well-being introduced a new aspect of study into travel research: savoring. Researchers didn't ask travelers only what activities they did, how long they were away, and how much sleep they got, they also asked participants how well they savored the experiences of travel. It defined *savoring* as "processes through which people actively derive pleasure and fulfillment in relation to positive experiences."[5]

The study checked in with fifty-four travelers before, during, and after their trips, which averaged twenty-three days. (A twenty-three–day vacation! Clearly, this was not an American study.) The results surprised and saddened me: For many, the boost that participants felt in health and

well-being during travel faded completely upon their return
to work. But good news lurked in the results. The travelers
who savored experiences were more likely to maintain well-
being boosts after they returned home. Savoring was more
important to long-term wellness than what people did on
vacation, who they were with, or how much they detached
from work. Savoring separates vacations (which end when
we get home) from retreats (which continue to benefit our
lives even after we unpack). Those who savored could be
fully where they were, while they were there. We can also
refer to savoring as mindfulness. Thoreau would call it paying attention.

Brein told me that savoring is a teachable skill. Learning to savor while traveling gives us the ultimate souvenir:
learning to savor our lives back home. So go, travel, see
the world—but if you're going to call it a retreat, be in the
moment and pay attention when you get there. And then,
do the same even after you return.

Retreat Lesson 2: Behold the Power of a Four-Day Break (Even at Home)

One randomized study in Germany compared four-night
staycations versus vacations. They sent forty middle man-
agers on vacation: Half stayed home, and half stayed in
a hotel in another town. The immediate effects were the
same for staycationers and vacationers—both groups

reported greater well-being and lowered stress. But getting away to a new place made the positive effects last longer. The mental health boost persisted an impressive forty-five days for the vacationers, while the boosts didn't last as long for those who stayed home.[6]

Compare this to the Dutch study, and it doesn't make sense initially. Why did both German groups maintain their post-vacation bliss while the Dutch vacationers returned to their pre-vacation baselines right away, even after much longer breaks? Researchers hypothesized that the strong response might've been due to another difference: the four-night trip. "It seems that short vacations of four nights are long enough to fully recover and short enough to limit the massive pile of work after return."

The researchers believe that a series of shorter retreats throughout the year may provide greater benefits to well-being than one long getaway. Brein supports the idea of short retreats. Even a staycation, when combined with savoring, can create lasting benefits. It's not about how far we go, but how attentive we become.

"Go to the Saturday markets, interact with the people in the mom-and-pop shops. Just take the time to smell the roses a little more, maybe by just breaking away a little bit from the home pattern and go and being a little more experimental where you live," he told me. "Some of the benefits carry over."

Retreat Lesson 3: The Right Travel Destination Makes Savoring Simpler

Even for close-to-home retreats, where we choose to go can set us up for greater benefits. Psychologist Stephan Kaplan analyzed where we should go to overcome "directed attention fatigue," when we're mentally exhausted by trying to focus on one thing while being pinged by multiple other distractions. ("Directed attention fatigue" may be a chronic ailment for most of us.) His study found that the ideal getaway environment should have the following:

- Fascination: Does it encourage us to be engaged without effort?
- Being away: Are we physically or mentally distanced from our usual routine?
- Extent: Is there enough going on to occupy our mind for the duration of the trip?
- Compatibility: Does the location fit with our personality?[7]

Interestingly, Thoreau checked all four boxes just a mile and a half from town. His journal is proof that he didn't need to travel far in order to savor. Each entry shows him fascinated by frogs, blooms, weather. He believed that a truly curious person could savor beauty everywhere, while a bore couldn't savor anything anywhere. "Where is 'Unexplored land' but in our own untried enterprises?" he wrote in a letter to a friend. "To an adventurous spirit any place— London, New York, Worcester, or his own yard, is 'unexplored land.' . . . To a sluggish & defeated spirit even the Great Basin & the Polaris are trivial places."

Sabbatical as the Ultimate Retreat

It's hard enough to plan a trip. It seems infinitely harder to plan—or even visualize—a sabbatical. That's why clients go to Katrina McGhee for sabbatical coaching. She works with people who seek advice about taking an extended break from work. McGhee helps them with the practical and philosophical elements of a sabbatical: how to save for one, what to do during one, how to handle fear of the unknown, how to return to professional life. McGhee said that for most of her clients, the hardest part isn't planning a sabbatical but giving themselves permission to discover who they are beyond work.

"My clients tend to be high achievers. Their whole lives, they've been trying to be the good person. They've been trying to win the accolades," she told me. "For them, [a sabbatical] isn't something reasonable people do."

Then again, not much about our current culture seems reasonable either, one in which we spend the most active and healthy years of our lives working and saving to take care of ourselves when we're old and sick. ("Why should they begin digging their graves as soon as they are born?" Thoreau wrote in a devastating line in *Walden*.) McGhee said that at some point, her clients all reach a point when they realize that they must fight for the experiences they want before it's too late. "You realize that no one is going to come along one day and tell you, 'Hey, you did a really good job at sacrificing your happiness all those years, so now we're going to give you the life you want,'" she said.

For some, a sabbatical is a temporary escape to enjoy the hobbies that work doesn't allow time for: writing that novel, traveling the world, hiking that mountain. For others, it's a period to reassess: Is this career the right one for me? McGhee also encourages clients to consider a third, radical option: that sabbatical may be about practicing the art of nothing.

"We have become people that define ourselves by output. 'How much did I do? Am I productive? Am I doing something? I have to be doing something! People have to see me as worthy.' And I hate that," McGhee said. "The essential part for me of a sabbatical is this intentional extended period of time where you remove yourself from the grind and the belief that you have to be productive to be worthy—really, really, rethinking your identity."

McGhee learned about sabbaticals when she took her own at thirty-two. On paper, she'd done everything right until then: She had an MBA and a secure job as a market researcher. Yet there was a gap between the person she knew she really was—adventurous, curious, spontaneous—and the predictable office life she lived. She had ideas and plans that lit her up inside, but her life didn't allow her the time to do them. "I realized, 'I'm not living a life that is mine,'" McGhee told me. "I realized, if I don't change anything, I'm going to blink, be sixty-five, retire, and wonder what the hell happened to my life."

McGhee decided to spend one year traveling the world and realizing her potential. But there was the pesky issue of money: She had just $1,500 in the bank and $50,000 in student loans. She created a sabbatical budget and began an aggressive two-year savings plan. When she hit her target of $40,000, she quit her job and began her adventure: a three-month road trip, seven months abroad, time home with family for the holidays. Even after she returned to the corporate world, the experience changed her; she was more confident, more willing to take a risk. She used her sabbatical as a differentiator, and it became the first thing potential employers wanted to discuss during interviews.

Within five weeks of returning, she had five job offers, and she accepted one for her dream job. Friends and colleagues asked about sabbaticals constantly, and within a few years, McGhee again saved up enough money for her next adventure: becoming a self-employed sabbatical coach. A publisher even contacted her to write a book about sabbaticals, *Taking a Career Break for Dummies*. She realized that her break didn't hamper her success but led to greater success than ever. "When you're doing what you feel to be true and using your gifts in a way that you want to use them, that's when you achieve crazy success," McGhee said.

Someone else said something remarkably similar. "I learned this, at least, by my experiment," Thoreau wrote at the end of *Walden*. "If one advances confidently in the direction of his dreams, and endeavors to live the life which he has imagined, he will meet with a success unexpected in common hours."

RECLAIMING THE SABBATICAL

Sabbaticals and gap years have been the privileged realms of academics and college kids for centuries. Anyone else who chose extended time off from the job got the harsh glare of judgment. Hard workers don't need breaks, right?

That's changed. More of us have begun to question our relationship to work. What do our jobs take from us? Do we really need to answer that email at 10:00 p.m.? Are the demands of this job compatible with a good life? Millions of workers decided they needed time off to figure that out.

In January 2022, about 6 percent of American workers began a sabbatical—twice the rate of previous years, according to an analysis by Gusto, a payroll processor. That year, sabbaticals became so common that LinkedIn introduced the option for users to declare career breaks in their profiles. The blog that announced LinkedIn's new feature cited a study that showed 35 percent of workers wanted to take a break at some point in their career. "As a talent acquisition professional for over twenty years, I've interviewed hundreds—maybe even thousands—of candidates, and more and more frequently I'm seeing people take much needed breaks from their careers," wrote Jennifer Shappley, LinkedIn's vice president of talent.[8]

Voluntary gaps in résumés were no longer scarlet letters. Some companies even began offering paid sabbaticals as career perks. Intel offers an eight-week sabbatical after seven years of service; Nike gives five weeks after ten years of service. More people were willing to take sabbaticals, even if their company didn't pay them or if it meant quitting. As these career breaks became more common, the stigma decreased when workers shared their stories. Time away was worth it. It may even be marketable.

"After sabbatical, you have the same experience, you have the same education, you have the same network. The only difference between you and every other person is that you have a shit ton more courage, that you have taken time out to recharge all of your batteries . . . versus the other people that have just been racing on the hamster wheel nonstop," McGhee told me.

The reasons behind sabbaticals vary widely. A study published in the *Harvard Business Review* followed fifty people who went on sabbatical.[9] It divided sabbaticals into three categories:

- Working holidays: People who wanted a break to relax
- Free dives: People who craved adventure and travel
- Quests: Burned-out workers whose mental or physical health were at risk without a break

The study found that "all sabbatical trajectories led to individuals feeling more affirmed upon their return." Whether the person returned to their job depended on which category they fell into. Most who took working holidays or free dives returned to their jobs or the same industry. Questers, naturally, sought new directions. The question shifted from "Is it risky to my professional life to take a sabbatical?" to "Is it riskier to my personal life not to take a sabbatical?"

SABBATICAL AS SURVIVAL STRATEGY

When I talk with Melissa and John Butler over Zoom, they're in a coffeeshop in Bali, tropical plants peeking from behind their shoulders.[10] The Butlers are two months into a year-long sabbatical with their two grade-school children. They came from Chicago, where they lived in a big house and made plenty of money in finance jobs. For Melissa, who grew up poor, it was the American dream. But the pressures of their careers and the desire to keep up with their neighbors took a toll: addiction, mental health struggles. "I felt like he was going to commit suicide or I was going to have a nervous breakdown," Melissa told me. "Something bad was going to happen."

After she and John began therapy, they decided to strip everything away to start fresh. They sold their house and almost all their possessions and began a year-long sabbatical in Bali. "I needed silence so I could hear myself," Melissa said. "I'm a great decision maker and have great intuition, but my life was too noisy."

In Bali, they live simply on very little money. Bali isn't a year-long vacation; Melissa says that they're there to save

their own lives. Like Thoreau, Melissa and John went somewhere they could minimize expenses and distractions to
learn what living well means to them.

"It's for us to take a step back from the job and focus
on family and focus on being more present and emotionally available," John said. "It's a little radical, a little wild.
It's living for the experience of living, as opposed to just
going through the motions of the corporate life I'd grown
so accustomed to."

John and Melissa have no post-Bali plan. They want
to rediscover who they are, reconnect as a family, and re-
store their well-being before they write their next chapter.
They've learned that a simple lifestyle requires just a fraction of their former incomes, and the international school
that their children attend costs less than the private schools
back home. There are easier ways to live, they've realized.
Maybe they won't even leave Bali at the end of the year.

John laughed when he told me that he no longer knows
how to introduce himself. A year ago, he had a label: He
was John, finance consultant. Now, he's not sure. And he
loves that.

"I don't want anything to do with those old labels any-
more," John said. "But it is interesting to try to figure out
what to say when I meet somebody. For now, it's just like,
'I'm on sabbatical and trying to figure out the next stage
of life.'" Or, as Thoreau might say, he's standing on the

meeting of two eternities, the past and future, which is precisely the present moment.

Five Questions:
Create Space from the World

1. What questions do you find hard to answer when you're surrounded by people and screens and notifications?
2. Do you find the idea of solitude to be liberating, intimidating, or both?
3. In what ways do you think differently when you're not within grabbing distance of your phone? Consider how you perceive time, how you focus, what you think about.
4. What would your dream retreat look like? Think of all the fun details: where it would be, how long you would stay there, who (if anyone) you'd bring along, and what you'd hope to learn about yourself during that time.
5. How can you insert small moments of separateness into your schedule? Consider all types of options: It could be going to a place (a separate room, a walk outdoors), creating a habit (digital sabbath, early mornings), or engaging in an activity (a solo jog, a meditation practice).

Embrace Your Inner Misfit

*To stand apart while standing tall
is a superpower.*

*I desire that there may be as many different persons in
the world as possible, but I would have each one be very
careful to find out and pursue his own way, and not his
father's or mother's or his neighbor's instead.*
—HENRY DAVID THOREAU

*If you're always trying to be normal, you will
never know how amazing you can be.*
—MAYA ANGELOU

Some people love to hate on Thoreau. Whether the criticism comes from his contemporaries or from people today on social media, it extends far beyond his writing style, his word choice, or his dedication to a pun. The criticism gets downright personal. Take, for example, this excerpt from a 1954 review of *Walden*: "It is difficult to understand that a mother had ever clasped this hermit to her bosom, that a sister had ever imprinted on his lips a tender kiss."[1]

Yikes, right? I mean, not everyone needs to love the book, but this seems needlessly harsh. It's not an unusual reaction to Thoreau, however. Here are more:

> For some reason, my generation preferred the puritanical Thoreau, a sorehead and loner whose clunky line about marching to your own drummer has found its way into a million graduation speeches. Thoreau tried to make a virtue out of lack of rhythm. . . . He wrote elegantly about independence and forgot to thank his mom for doing his laundry. —Garrison Keillor, *The New York Times*

> And yet we made a classic of the book, and a moral paragon of its author—a man whose deepest desire and signature act was to turn his back on the rest of us. —Kathryn Schulz, "Pond Scum," *The New Yorker*

> Thoreau was an antisocial asshole, a liar, and Walden
> Pond was a 20-minute walk from his mom's place.
> —@calebbhannan, X

Most Thoreau criticism boils down to this: What a weirdo! Who did this guy think he was? It's a curious amount of anger toward a man whose actions harmed no one. The guy lived in a cabin by himself for a couple years; he didn't tie up traffic on I-95 during rush hour. Here's the real problem: Thoreau dared to be his own person, and he dared others to be, too. The very reason fans love Thoreau—because he was willing to be different—is the reason others criticize Thoreau.

It's easy to mock a misfit, but it's much braver to be one. However, society moves at the speed of misfits. Think of the visionaries you respect in any field; their greatness results from a willingness to be different, to take a risk on themselves. Think of Steve Jobs, a college dropout who tinkered with computers in the garage of his parents' house; think of John Waters, a Baltimore misfit who honed his artistry through performing violent puppet shows for neighbors; think of a skinny kid named Stephen Curry who insisted on shooting baskets from beyond the three-point line. Misfits change the norms, remake the rules, and change how we see the world and even ourselves. People who stick with the crowd may win more acceptance during their lifetimes, but they're less likely to leave a legacy beyond them.

Thoreau got an early start being different, which often happens to poor kids who can't afford to fit in, even if they wanted. He went to Harvard—"You have barely got in," the college president ever-so-helpfully told him upon his acceptance—on a scholarship for promising yet disadvantaged students. Back then, Harvard required all students to wear black coats. The college penalized any student who didn't wear the standard black coat, except Thoreau, who wore a green one. Administrators likely understood that the scholarship kid from Concord couldn't afford another coat, so they turned a blind eye to this infraction. But I think about Thoreau walking around Harvard during those four years. Not only was Thoreau the poor kid on campus, he was the poor kid in a green coat. The thing is, I can't imagine he minded.

Instead of trying to fit in, Thoreau lived his life being, figuratively, the guy in a green coat in a sea of black coats. Thoreau believed that if someone looked like everyone else, whether in their appearance or in their life choices, they missed out on the chance to discover who they were and what they were capable of. The world has plenty of everyone-elses out there already.

We only know Thoreau today because he held onto his misfit status. It's the reason students still read *Walden* in English classes and why thousands of people make pilgrimages to Walden Pond. Thoreau could've been a normal, respectable Concordian who won the respect of his neighbors with a steady job and mortgaged farm. Instead, he went his own way, and people today—175 years later—remain in awe of something that seems so simple: a person who insisted on being himself.

The willingness to be different, to risk authenticity in a world that rewards conformity, requires confidence and bravery. It's easy to think that any idea adopted by the crowd must be better than one we'd come up with on our own. "Our will to doubt can be just as powerfully sapped by an internal sense that societal conventions must have a sound basis, even if we are not sure exactly what this may be, because they have been adhered to by a great many people for a long time," wrote Alain de Botton in *The Consolations of Philosophy*. "We stifle our doubts and follow the flock because we cannot conceive of ourselves as pioneers of hitherto unknown, difficult truths."

"Pioneer of hitherto unknown, difficult truths"—what a fantastic way to describe Thoreau. And what a fantastic title to aspire to.

Thoreau wrote *Walden* as a misfit, for other misfits. In her excellent biography *Henry David Thoreau: A Life*, Laura Dassow Walls wrote, "Thoreau knew plenty of town scoffers sneered at him behind his back, but he also knew that dreamers and 'poor students' like him too often lived in quiet desperation. To all the others—not just the scoffers but the 'strong and valiant' natures who relish things as they are—he asked only that, should they try on the coat that is *Walden*, they not 'stretch the seams' lest they ruin it for those whom it fits." Green coats aren't for everyone, after all.

Thoreau didn't seek to be different for the sake of being different. He wanted to live a life that was authentic to his personality and his priorities, and he wanted to befriend fellow misfits who lived original and authentic lives, too. Thoreau makes us wonder: Why does it seem so brave to risk being oneself? How many of our decisions are dictated by societal expectation more than personal preference? And what kind of life can we live if we prioritize experience over reputation?

Benefits of Being a Misfit

Misfits may not win universal approval, but they may gain something better. Being a misfit can make a person more creative, even happier. Misfits can make better financial decisions, too. The willingness to be different and to resist the pull of conformity can lead to a lifetime of wise and interesting choices.

"Much like what psychology suggests, your unusualness is a fabric woven from the thread of your life," wrote Olga Khazan in *Weird*. "Your identity, your environment, and your experiences all combine to make you who you are. But your weirdness is also a hint at what you might live to see and do, at what hidden powers you possess."

And who doesn't feel weird at times? More than a quarter of American adults feel that other people rarely or never understand them, according to a Cigna Group survey.

We've got two choices then: To see our weirdness as an obstacle to acceptance or to let our weirdness point us to adventures ahead. If we realize the potential that weirdness brings, then weirdness becomes our superpower, Khazan argues. It's about how we perceive our differences that matters more than how others perceive them: "Public opinion is a weak tyrant compared with our own private opinion," Thoreau wrote. "What a man thinks of himself, that is which determines, or rather indicates, his fate."

Creative people tend to be weirdos and misfits. A study of one thousand renowned creative professionals—the likes of Frida Kahlo and Jean-Paul Sartre—revealed that they were much more likely to have been considered "odd or peculiar" as kids or "different" as adults than their peers who entered traditional fields like business or the military. Imagine what would've happened—or wouldn't have happened—if they prioritized fitting in over embracing their uniqueness.

Misfits even spark originality among noncreative types: When a group has a member who's a nonconformist, that group will create more ideas and more imaginative ideas than a group of like-minded people. Misfits are the heart of innovation, art, and progress. And they can even spark confidence to inspire others to become misfits. Originality, somewhat ironically, can be contagious.

Why, then, do so many people within a society look so similar? At a time when we have access to all kinds of thinkers, all types of ideas, why do so many of us make the same life choices during the same life stages? Blame insecurity, a powerful driver of conformity. If we feel unsure about our decisions (and who doesn't?), it can feel safer to keep pace with the crowd rather than pull out on one's own and risk being alone and wrong—or worse, alone and weird.

CULPRIT OF CONFORMITY 1: STATUS ANXIETY

Economics, oddly, may be partly to blame for killing individualism. The pull of conformity may be stronger now than in recent memory, partly due to the widened gap between rich and poor. In countries that claim to be meritocracies, many people conclude that the wealthy must be smarter and harder working, to have "deserved" their success, while everyone else must not be trying enough. The Horatio Alger, up-by-your-bootstrap fable refuses to die. Today, the gap between rich and poor stretches wider than ever. The bottom 50 percent of American households have less than 2 percent of the country's wealth, while the top 10 percent hold almost three-quarters of it. That's a lot of people looking up, wondering where they went wrong.

The result is status anxiety. Status anxiety compels us to acquire things, from homes to clothes to personalities that make us seem more like those we deem successful. By mimicking the lives of those at the top, we try to feel more worthy—to others as well as to ourselves. "It is the luxurious and dissipated who set the fashions which the herd so diligently follow," Thoreau wrote.

Status anxiety not only makes us feel lacking, but it makes us act impulsively. A study showed that when people feel a lack of power, they are more willing to pay higher prices for items associated with status—to fake it until they make it, even as they drain their bank accounts.[2] Purchases driven by shame become dangerous, not only to our mental well-being but also to our financial well-being. When people buy things to quell status anxiety, they're more likely to be in debt, they're more likely to have longer commutes, and they're more likely to get trapped into cycles of unsustainable consumption.[3] Pretending to be richer makes people poorer and less happy.

"Capitalism thrives on bad feelings. . . . Discontented people buy more stuff," wrote Astra Taylor, author of *The Age of Insecurity: Coming Together as Things Fall Apart*. Taylor calls this "manufactured insecurity," when brands persuade us to feel shame about something neutral—wrinkles, the make of a car, the style of jeans—to compel us to buy something we don't need to fix what isn't broken. In a 2023 Instagram post, actor Jameela Jamil noted how refreshed she felt to spend time in Europe, where women "have wrinkles and facial expressions." At home in Los Angeles, Jamil wrote that "everyone here is starting to morph into the same face. And I understand why. We have beauty rules set for us, and we all, myself included, feel this underlying pressure to conform."

This pressure to conform worsens as we compare ourselves with people in higher income brackets. Sociologists call this the "vertical expansion of our reference group."[4] Before social media and reality TV, we kept up with the Joneses next door. Now, we keep up with the Kardashians. The people in the bottom 90 percent can peek into the lives of the top 10 percent—the brands they prefer, the luxuries they enjoy—and it's tempting to want those things, too. But there's a problem. When we don't share the same income level, one person's little splurge is another person's economic shackle. Or, as journalist Robert Quillen defined it: "Americanism: Using money you haven't earned to buy things you don't need to impress people you don't like."[5]

CULPRIT OF CONFORMITY 2: ALGORITHMS

During an age when the assembly lines of factories replaced the individual work of craftsmen, Thoreau worried that people would soon mimic machines. ("He has no time to be anything but a machine," he wrote of working people in the era of industrialization.) What Thoreau didn't foresee, however, was the dystopian plot twist of the 2020s: that people would one day need to curry favor with machines to communicate with other people. Algorithms have become arbiters of taste and gatekeepers of connection. If someone has a message they want to share—a piece of art, of writing, of music, of activism—they must win over the algorithms of social media to reach their audiences. "It builds to a sense that, since we users cannot control the technology, we may as well succumb to the limits of algorithmic culture and view it as inevitable," wrote Kyle Chayka in *Filterworld: How Algorithms Flattened Culture*. What meets the algorithm's rules gains momentum, so "the popular becomes more popular, and the obscure becomes even less visible."

When the internet was in its infancy, it held the potential to democratize art and media. A newbie writer could blog as easily as a famous author could. There was hope that the misfits would rise. Now, however, artists and writers face a choice: Serve the algorithm or risk irrelevancy. The algorithm doesn't prioritize weird or quirky thinkers; it uplifts what already works and promotes those willing to conform to its rules. "Men have become the tools of their tools," Thoreau wrote.

The result is that it becomes harder for us to develop our unique taste; to learn what we appreciate in art, music, books, and fashion; to dig into the weird stuff. Algorithms reduce the friction in our search for art and ideas, but friction is an essential part of what we need to fine-tune our individual taste. Otherwise, we become passive consumers of content that's been machine-approved for the masses. "We are free to choose anything," Chayka wrote. "Yet the choice we often make is to not have a choice, to have our purview shaped by automatic feeds." Instead of bin diving in record stores for albums, we let Spotify choose based on what we've already heard. Instead of walking the aisles in Blockbuster looking for a movie, we choose from titles that Netflix suggests based on who it thinks we are. Instead of seeking inspiration from friends, we look to influencers who have already played and won the algorithm game. We consume more of the same, just as everyone else consumes more of the same—which can mean death to our inner misfit.

THE COST OF CONFORMITY

When we resemble everyone else in our appearance, choices, and tastes, we lose more than our money. We lose ourselves. "Imitation is suicide," Ralph Waldo Emerson wrote in "Self-Reliance." This is the take-away from the famous 1951 group-think study that showed that people would rather belong to a group that's wrong than to stand on their own and be right. Researcher Solomon Asch asked subjects to match the length of a line on one card to the length of a line on another card with multiple lines. The answer was obvious, and it was intended to be. When subjects were asked to match lines, they guessed right more than 99 percent of the time—if they guessed alone. But when seven actors, pretending to be fellow test subjects, guessed the wrong answer first, 32 percent of subjects guessed wrong, too, so their answer would align with the others'. In follow-up interviews, some subjects admitted that they knew they had guessed wrong, but they preferred to belong to a group of people who were wrong than to be correct on their own.

Do you think we're braver and less conformist today? Unfortunately not. People on both sides of the political spectrum will share fake news (even if they know it's fake) to gain approval from their social circles, according to research published by the American Psychological Association. "Political ideology alone doesn't explain people's tendency to share fake news within their social groups," said lead researcher Matthew Asher Lawson in a story on the group's website. "There are many factors at play, including the very basic desire to fit in and not to be excluded."

Behold the power of being a misfit: to fight the pull of status anxiety and conformity means nothing short of freedom. To develop individual taste, not dictated by algorithms or brands. To make life choices based on our values, even when they don't match everyone else's. To have the courage to show the world who we are and what we know to be right. To be an original. Thoreau lived a life showing everyone who he really was, reputation be damned. To be a misfit begins with a strong sense of self, and it helps us notice the tricks that lure us into conformist choices and unwise purchases—and then to decide if they're worth the cost, in the Waldenomics sense.

Dress Like a Misfit

It won't shock you to learn that Thoreau wasn't exactly a fashionista. Thoreau—deeply practical Thoreau—cared little how he looked, wearing outdated clothes that were likely dirty and torn from his nature walks. Brent Ranalli, who gives presentations as Thoreau in biographically authentic outfits, told me, "He definitely wore corduroys because they were not fashionable. He took pride in going his own way." Thoreau marveled at people who would rather walk to town with a broken leg than a torn pant leg, or how people paid more attention to how they looked than how they lived. "I am sure that there is greater anxiety, commonly, to have fashionable, or at least clean and unpatched clothes, than to have a sound conscience," Thoreau wrote.

Those college years of being the poor kid in a green coat left their mark on young Henry. Being the oddball—and not just surviving the experience but making friends throughout it—offers courage to be the oddball again.

One of my favorite moments in *Walden* is the story of Thoreau's visit to a tailor to get his clothes altered. It's a complete clash of cultures resulting in two people who can barely understand each other. The tailor attempted to talk Thoreau out of the style he requested: "They do not make them so now," she warned him, hoping to save her customer from embarrassment. Thoreau couldn't be convinced. He wrote that the tailor was "not emphasizing the 'They' at all, as if she quoted an authority as impersonal as the Fates." You can picture the stand-off: On one side, a woman whose job is to adapt clothes to fit the current fashions; on the other, a customer who hated nothing more than conformity. But Thoreau made an excellent point: Who they heck are "they" anyway? And what do "they" have to do with him—or with any of us? Whenever I hear a fact attributed to what "they" say or what "they" wear this season, I picture a confused Thoreau just trying to make his clothes comfortable, if perhaps a little dorky. Fashion, to Thoreau, was about conformity: "The head monkey at Paris puts on a traveller's cap, and all the monkeys in America do the same," he wrote.

It tempting to hear this and think that this is where Thoreau lived up to his grumpy reputation. And, to be fair, Thoreau—especially as he stood in the tailor's shop wearing his torn, outdated pants and a baffled expression— could probably be a bit of a crank at times. But you'll see his true gripe isn't just with the pace of trends but with the economics of fashion: "The principal object is, not that mankind may be well and honestly clad, but, unquestionably, that the corporations may be enriched." This is about much more than clothes. This is about capitalism. In addition to fighting conformity, Thoreau tells consumers that fashion is a sham trying to get us to spend our money to enrich companies that don't need any more of it. He was willing to be a misfit to avoid becoming a cog in an unjust machine that kept workers locked in horrible conditions for sub-livable wages. It was a fairly new fight. It was during Thoreau's generation when textiles shifted from hand-crafted goods to mass-produced products. Instead of artisans making a good living in textiles, people—often, young immigrant women—suffered in poverty even as they churned out clothes in factories. Thoreau wanted people to stop and think: Why should we enrich unethical companies to buy things we don't need?

This situation has grown worse in our era of fast fashion and social media. Pressure to buy more clothes and adopt new trends has intensified with influencers, who earn followers and fame the more they convince people to shop and to look just like they do. ("Influencing runs on jealousy," Chayka wrote.) Trends change more quickly, too. For centuries, fashions—fabrics, hem lines, silhouettes—could last twenty years or more. Now, there aren't just trends but microtrends—coastal grandmother, eclectic grandpa, and dark academia—that go in and out of style within three to six months.

Today, people wear 20 percent of their clothes 80 percent of the time, according to the *Wall Street Journal*. On average, people wear an item about ten times before throwing it out, and they buy 60 percent more clothes than they did just 15 years ago.[6] Yet consumption of clothes is expected to increase. Fast fashion means we can buy cheap clothes and lots of them, and only wearing items a few times (or not at all) doesn't come at a big cost—to us, at least. To textile workers and to the environment, the effects are devastating.

Factory conditions haven't improved much since Thoreau's age. Today, 98 percent of people around the world who make clothes do not earn a livable wage. That's nearly 75 million people who remain in poverty despite their employment in an in-demand industry.[7] In addition to this labor nightmare, the clothing industry creates an ecological disaster. About 10 percent percent of global CO_2 emissions come from the fashion industry. Nearly 90 percent of clothes will wind up in an incinerator or in a landfill, according to the World Bank.

In a Waldenomics sense, that trendy $20 fast-fashion top has a true cost far higher than its price tag. The bad news is that that top just makes us look like everyone else; the worse news is, we hurt a lot of people to look that way.

FIGHTING FAST FASHION

Modern-day Thoreaus beg shoppers to consider alternatives. They ask us to sit out trends and to purchase from thrift stores or to avoid new purchases to rent clothes from sites like Rent the Runway. They remind us that by opting out of fast fashion, we can dress like a misfit but live like an activist.

Another strategy is to invest more money in fewer items that are responsibly made and last longer. By resisting the trend of the moment ("dark academia" came and went before I knew it was a thing, and I survived), we can create a style all our own while not supporting unfair labor practices or contributing to waste. One strategy is the #30Wears campaign, the brainchild of climate activist Olivia Firth. The rule is simple if not easy: One doesn't buy a piece of clothing unless they can imagine wearing it thirty times. The goal is to ward off disposable fashion and to think of investing in quality pieces that will last in one's closet—not the landfill.

"We only have one planet and we're using three planets' worth of resources," Firth said in an CNBC interview. "Looking at fashion, we have a huge problem. The brands are trying to protect their business, but in fact, the businesses need to protect people who make the fashion."

Another strategy is the capsule wardrobe. The idea is to create a season's worth of outfits with a handful of high-quality items that coordinate well, maximizing outfit potential and longevity of pieces. Courtney Carver started Project 333, a capsule wardrobe challenge of creating three months' worths of outfits with thirty-three items (this includes accessories and shoes, but it does not include pajamas or workout clothes). Items that are worn out or don't fit well can be replaced, but the idea is to sit out trends and stick with one's personal style. You might not look like everyone else, but you'll always look like you.

Melissa Russell of the Simple Lionheart Life blog told me that adopting a capsule wardrobe has not only helped her bank account and the planet, it's also made her enjoy clothes more. "I don't ever feel like I'm missing out with a simplified wardrobe," she told me. "When you wear clothes you love and feel great in, it's not so tempting to try every trend that comes along. I'd rather stick to what I know I love, knowing dressing this way always makes me feel confident and good about myself."

Going against the grain to be somewhat of a fashion misfit—being willing to hold onto last year's look and not jump on this season's trend—can even make a day easier. With fewer choices come fewer decisions. President Barack Obama told *Vanity Fair* that he minimized his wardrobe by only wearing gray or blue suits: "I'm trying to pare down decisions," he said. "Because I have too many other decisions to make." (And just remember the mocking headlines President Obama made when he defied his clothing minimalism and opted for a tan suit: "The Audacity of Taupe," "Yes, We Tan!")

Joshua Becker of Becoming Minimalist also adopted a capsule wardrobe to minimize his decisions. He's got about thirty-five or forty things in his closet, mostly black v-necks, some black long-sleeved shirts, a few button-ups. When he needs to replace one, he simply replaces it with another of the same. He knows the brands he likes, the stores that carry them. I asked him if he ever feels as though he misses out on new trends, and he said no right away.

"I don't want to sound prideful, but no, I'm kind of proud that I have a style and that I'm not wavering back and forth with fashion," he replied. "I think we should be more embarrassed about having a closet full of clothes that we don't wear than we typically are. Because really, what is that but wasteful spending and wasted time and trying to impress people or keep up with fashion, so we buy a bunch of stuff we don't need?"

Live Like a Misfit

To Thoreau's neighbors, the decision that propelled him into full-fledged misfit status was his choice of a home. His nature obsession seemed a little weird to them; his inability to stick with a job was off-putting. But for a Harvard grad to move into a homemade cabin in the woods and live alone there? That's kooky misfit material.

Here's a bit of literary trivia: In *Walden*, Thoreau rarely refers to his building at the pond as a cabin—only twice. To him, it was his house, his dwelling. He called it home.

Thoreau spends a lot of time pondering the idea of home in *Walden*. What do we really need in a home? How many people really think about what they need in a home before they choose one? "Most men appear never to have considered what a house is, and are actually though needlessly poor all their lives because they think that they must have such a one as their neighbours have."

During Thoreau's life, the popularity of the home lifestyle magazine took off, showcasing beautifully decorated rooms and high-end architectural designs. Today, these magazines would be like *House Beautiful* or *Architectural Digest*. Suddenly, the home became an extension of self, an expression of wealth and status. It wasn't just a place to live but also a thing to show off.

Considering the debt that his neighbors acquired to have such a home, Thoreau wondered: At what point is a dwelling more about impressing people outside the home than housing those within it? At what point does a person no longer own a house, but the house owns them? "Our houses are such unwieldy property," Thoreau wrote, "that we are often imprisoned rather than housed in them."

How much have we been socialized into our belief of what a home should be? What if we thought less about the appearance of a home and more about the experience within—and beyond—it?

A reckoning of home is happening now, sparked by necessity but fueled by creativity. The American Dream of a single-family home is increasingly out of reach, especially to Gen Z and Millennial adults who've faced a steep increase in the costs of higher education, childcare, and real estate. Not only is this goal out of reach financially, it also seems to be out of touch practically. Perhaps we're not intended to live this way, cut off from others by fences and yards and so much distance. With historical context, it's clear that Westerners are the true misfits when it comes to the idea of a home. In our society, the "neolocal residence" looms as the ideal, one in which a nuclear family lives in a separate home on property they own. For most of human history, this wasn't the case. Extended networks of families shared property, creating large networks of kin that shared caretaking of children, the elderly, the sick, and the poor. The hyperindividualistic way we do things now isn't just fairly recent, it's the mark of a society that's WEIRD—western, educated, industrialized, rich, and democratic—according to Joseph Henrich's *The WEIRDest People in the World: How the West Became Psychologically Peculiar and Particularly Prosperous*.

Now, more people are starting a discussion: What exactly does a home need to be? Is the most valuable part of the home the room inside it, the yard around it, or the community beyond it? In *Everyday Utopia*, Kristen R. Ghodsee

makes a compelling argument for choice C: community.
Ghodsee believes that the reason so many people remember college as the best years of their lives has less to do
with youth and more to do with campus living. For four (or
five) years, people live surrounded by thousands of people
their age, within walking distance of places to meet for cof-
fee, drinks, or impromptu frisbee games. Most college cam-
puses are cohousing, pedestrian-friendly utopias. Thoreau
believed a conformist view of home can make us needlessly
poor, but Ghodsee adds another consideration: Can a conformist idea of home make us needlessly lonely, too?

Why do so many people trade this social utopian living for cul-de-sac suburbia, spread apart from the people
and places they enjoy? "How did so many of us find our
way into spaces rented from faceless landlords or contained
within privately owned but mortgaged walls that separate
us from our neighbors and mire us in debt?" Ghodsee wrote.
"When we search for a place to live, do we ever stop to
consider what our ideal living arrangements may be, or just
scan the listings for a decent place in a desirable neighbor-
hood that we can afford?"

TAKING THE BEST OF COLLEGE LIVING INTO ADULT LIFE

More misfits now envision home as a communal existence
that defies the standards of their culture. They wonder,

What if we could take the best parts of campus life and apply them to the most challenging aspects of adult life? "Now is the time to 'think different,'" Ghodsee wrote.

In a suburb north of London, twenty-six misfits have done just this. They're women between fifty and ninety-four years old, and they've turned an apartment building into a cohousing utopia. Within this building, each woman has her own apartment, as well as access to a common room where they meet for weekly dinners, yoga classes, and movie nights. Together, they tend to a vegetable and flower garden out back, and they pitch in on the building's maintenance and cleaning duties. These women have their own space, but they live surrounded by friends in a community they love. Men are allowed to come, but only to visit. "We have brothers, fathers, sons, grandsons, lovers and everything in between. The only thing is they can't come and live here," said Jude Tisdall, age seventy-one, in a story in *The Guardian*.

At a time when seniors face an epidemic of loneliness, cohousing like this seems like a brilliant alternative. These women have re-created college sorority life in their middle-aged and senior years, with all the friendships and none of the exams.

While the news often focuses on the loneliness epidemic among seniors, this isn't the loneliest demographic. The loneliest people today are young adults and parents, especially mothers and single parents, according to a Cigna

Group survey. It's natural, then, that the cohousing movement has become a draw to young families. Families have
a "postvaccine nostalgia for the pandemic pod," wrote Judith Shulevitz in a piece for *The New York Times*. During the
pandemic, some families united to share childcare duties
and schooling, briefly re-creating the "it takes a village" approach that is talked about but rarely achieved here.

Shulevitz toured Eastern Village, a cohousing community in Silver Spring, Maryland, that aims to be a solution
to the isolation of young families. It's a fifty-five-unit apartment building where each family has their own apartment,
but they share access to amenities like group dining rooms,
kids' playrooms, shared closets full of sports equipment and
baby furnishings, and quiet rooms for adults. About a hundred people live there, and most cite parenting as the top
reason. In Eastern Village, parents help watch each other's
kids and pitch in on babysitter costs. Meanwhile, kids have
plenty of safe spaces to play with their neighbors just down
the hall or upstairs. It's hard to imagine a kid wanting to
trade this life, with freedom and friends, for a fenced-in
yard. The parents benefit from the social environment, too.
"On any Wednesday or Saturday, a sociable soul can find a
neighbor to share a snack or a beer with," Shulevitz wrote.

Cohousing communities like these have been common
in Scandinavian countries for generations, but now people in the United States realize what they lost when they

gained square footage. Americans who choose cohousing communities may be today's misfits, but they might also be tomorrow's visionaries of a better system—and even bring a sense of more kinship-oriented cultures to the West. Shulevitz hopes that cohousing communities might show traditional neighborhoods what they're missing—and what they need to be true communities: "the least inspiration we can take from [cohousing] is to make our housing stock more varied, less focused on the nuclear family, so that members of extended families and groups of friends can be there for one another, too."

GOING TINY TO GAIN MORE

Austin is a fantastic city to visit—the lake, the live music, the tacos—but it's a pricey place to live. The median monthly rent is higher than the national average, at $2,125, according to Zillow.[8] Yet one woman, Carly DeFelice, has found a way to spend just one-third of that average rent to call Austin home.

DeFelice, thirty-eight, returned from a job sabbatical forever changed. Before her sabbatical, she felt burned out from work; during her career break, she realized how good freedom felt. There was no going back her old ways, DeFelice said in a 2023 story on CNBC. Even after she returned to working life, flexibility would be her top priority. Instead of finding an apartment to buy or rent, DeFelice paid

$14,000 for a used RV. This RV is now her home, wherever it's parked. She lives in this RV in Austin, and each month, she pays $750 for parking and about $42 for utilities.

DeFelice's RV is no frills: no dishwasher, no bathtub, no washer or dryer. But she gets to live in one of the most popular cities in the country for a fraction of what everyone else does, and she owns a place that she can take with her when she leaves. And, if she moves, she can lower her expenses even more. Before Austin, DeFelice lived in South Carolina, where her monthly parking fee was just $350. Imagine if your housing cost less than $5,000 a year; imagine how that would change your life, the options that would open. DeFelice trades amenities for freedom, and to her, it's total Waldenomics profit. "I felt so empowered getting that tow hitch, attaching it to my SUV and just hitting the road," DeFelice said in the story. "There's an amazing sense of freedom and adventure and thrill that I could not explain unless you've actually done that."[9]

Then, of course, there are tiny homes. A tiny home ranges between 100 and 400 square feet (Thoreau's Walden home was 150 square feet), and it can be built on a trailer or foundation. The average cost of a tiny home is $52,000, which is 87 percent less than the cost of an average home. About 68 percent of tiny homeowners do not have a mortgage.[10] It's an increasingly attractive option as housing continues to grow less affordable. Buying a traditional home can require sacrifice in all other areas of life, and more people question how much that home is worth it.

"So many relatives or friends . . . are now stuck, literally stuck in a full-time job to pay their accommodation," said a twenty-seven-year-old woman named Petra in a study about tiny house owners. "[They're] getting all stressed out and can't even invest in their well-being, their creativity, and they still also can't buy a house."[11]

In that same study, a thirty-seven-year-old woman named Amy in Oregon offered a tour of her tiny house, where she watches the stars from her bed through a skylight. Before the tiny home, she spent more than half of her income on apartment rent; now, she pays a farmer a nominal fee to park on his land. She enjoys her environmentally friendly lifestyle, and she values the flexibility to move her home when she wants to relocate for work or to live near family. Amy says the trade of square footage for freedom was well worth it, even if her house looks different from most everyone else's.

"Whenever I go back to the tiny house . . . I just cry because I am just so incredibly grateful," Amy said. "It feels like this secret that people don't know about. I'm like, if only you knew, you would change your life radically today, if you understood that this level of peace exists."

Five Questions:
Embrace Your Inner Misfit

1. Do you know anyone who has an especially strong sense of self and who can easily resist following the crowd? Think about what traits they have that set them apart from the crowd and what risks and rewards they reap from their individualism.

2. Without the influence of "them," what activities or purchases would you trade for time or money for yourself? Think about how you might dress, where you might live, or how your routine might change.

3. If you could dream up the ideal living arrangement for yourself, what would it be? Consider where it would be, who it would be with (or near), and what lifestyle it would allow you to have.

4. What are the pros and cons of living in your dream city in a nontraditional living arrangement (cohousing, tiny house, RV) versus living in an OK-enough city in a more traditional home?

5. What percent of your clothes do you wear 80 percent of the time?

Know What You Work For

*Know when and why to take a job,
and when and why to quit one.*

*The incessant anxiety and strain of some is a well-nigh
incurable form of disease. We are made to exaggerate
the importance of what work we do.*
—HENRY DAVID THOREAU

*Never get so busy making a living
that you forget to make a life.*
—DOLLY PARTON

Some critics paint Thoreau as a privileged Ivy League grad without financial obligations. Not so. He grew up in poverty, his family moving from one rented house to the next as his father flailed in business. During college, Thoreau took breaks for thirteen weeks at a time to work as a tutor to earn tuition money and caught up with his class when he returned. When his father's factory suffered a fire, he paid the bill. When his mom needed a home that would double as a boarding house for additional income, he contributed to the down payment. Thoreau lived his life worrying about money and how to make enough of it.

Thoreau was no purist. While we hail him as the country's greatest nature writer, the career that funded his writing may be the last one we'd expect: land surveyor. His surveying work resolved land disputes and even led to development at a time when logging destroyed his beloved woods at a rapid pace. Why did he do it? For the same reason most of us work: the money.

Thoreau sold out wisely, however. Surveying meant he could pay his bills while tapping into his mind for math and his love for the outdoors. It was a decently paying job— much better paying than writing—and it kept him outside, wandering fields and woods while wearing muddy boots and talking with his neighbors. While he knew that a business job would offer faster profit, Thoreau worried it would've distracted his focus: "I have tried trade; but I found that it would take ten years to get under way in that, and that then I should probably be on my way to the devil." One day, a surveying gig led him past Walden Pond, and he stopped at the site of his old cabin. It was then he decided to finish the book he began there. Ironically, it was Thoreau's work as a land surveyor that led him to publish *Walden*, eight years after he left the cabin.

Thoreau learned how to sell out strategically, to make money without destroying his soul. And, more importantly, he learned when and why to quit a job to begin another. He honed those skills at Walden Pond. "I left the woods for as good a reason as I went there," he wrote. "Perhaps it seemed to me that I had several more lives to live, and could not spend any more time for that one." It's the ultimate resignation letter.

Thoreau, the Quitter

Quitting is crucial to the story of Thoreau's professional life. We know Thoreau as a writer because his neighbors knew him as a quitter. Thoreau's journey from writer to surveyor back to writer (with many stops between) involved lots of quitting, and it can inspire us to quit more, too.

Thoreau's professional path began with teaching. He and his brother ran the Concord Academy for four years, but when his brother died, the heartbroken Thoreau closed the school. After that, Thoreau didn't choose a career but pieced together gigs: the town handyman, an assistant editor, a fencepost digger, a tutor, a land surveyor, and even a manure shoveler. When business at his father's pencil factory faltered, Thoreau worked there, too. Each job supported him in his preferred occupation: writer. But writing didn't pay well then (and not much has changed since), hence the surveying and fencepost digging.

His choices baffled the people of Concord. Here was Thoreau, a poor kid who scored a scholarship to Harvard— the only one of the four Thoreau kids to go to college— and then he blew his shot at making something of himself after graduation. While his fellow alumni pursued prestigious fields like finance, education, and the ministry, there was Thoreau, shoveling poop for a paycheck, just so he could get back to writing.

This doesn't mean that Thoreau lacked success. He excelled at each job. When he taught, he was among Concord's best-paid and most-loved teachers. (One student, Louisa May Alcott, became smitten with her teacher, and some believe he inspired her character of Laurie in *Little Women*.) When he worked in his dad's pencil factory, Thoreau's improvements to the graphite process made the Thoreau pencil the highest-quality pencil in the country. When Emerson asked Thoreau to be his family's substitute head of household and his children's tutor while he toured Europe, things went better than Emerson probably hoped. (Thoreau recalled a conversation with Emerson's son: "He very seriously asked me the other day—'Mr. Thoreau,—will you be my father?'") Thoreau could've spent his life as a successful teacher, pencil maker, or tutor. But instead, he quit.

The challenge for Thoreau was that he needed more from a job than being good at it. After Thoreau extracted what he desired from an experience, he moved on to the next opportunity. In his eulogy for Thoreau, Emerson wrote, "He declined to give up his large ambition of knowledge and action for any narrow craft or profession, aiming at a much more comprehensive calling, the art of living well."

Never one to conform, Thoreau reveled in his unconventional attitude toward a career. When Harvard sent a survey in 1847 asking alumni for professional updates, Thoreau toyed with them in his answer. He sent this reply: "I am a Schoolmaster, a Private Tutor, a Surveyor - a Gardener, a Farmer - a Painter, I mean a House Painter, a Carpenter, a Mason, a Day-Laborer, a Pencil-Maker, a Glass-paper Maker, a Writer, and sometimes a Poetaster." (A poetaster is a writer of bad poetry.) You can imagine the Harvard alumni committee rolling their eyes and regretting they ever asked.

Shortly after Thoreau returned to town from Walden Pond, however, a shift occurred in his career strategy. This change was likely caused by the very thing that inspires many sudden career moves. Thoreau needed money, lots of money—fast.

This is when Thoreau's shift from gig work to surveying happens. His first book deal was a precarious one. After having a hard time finding a publisher for *A Week on the Concord and Merrimack Rivers*, he agreed to risky terms: The publisher would print 1,000 copies of his book, but Thoreau had to promise to buy whatever copies didn't sell. His book sold just 294 copies. This is the joke behind the line in his journal that "I have now a library of nearly 900 volumes, over 700 of which I wrote myself."

Thoreau owed the publisher $290 to buy those remaining 706 books—about a year's salary for him. As a fellow writer, I can attest: Writing is a horrible way to make lots of money quickly. He shifted his focus to the skill that paid more than the rest: land surveying. Thoreau was an adept surveyor, and he enjoyed the work well enough. While at Walden, he surveyed the pond (length, width, and depth, too) just for fun. "His intimate knowledge of the territory about Concord, made him drift into the profession of land-surveyor," Emerson wrote of Thoreau. "His accuracy and skill in his work were readily appreciated, and he found all the employment he wanted."

Was surveying Thoreau's dream job? Not at all. Thoreau wasn't nearly as enamored with his surveying work as his neighbors were. In his journal, he griped that the jobs that required his greatest brainpower (writing and lecturing) paid the least. Meanwhile, the job that others could do just as well (surveying) paid the most. Artists and musicians who make a living by working in restaurants and offices today can relate to his frustration. In his journal during one of his most active years for surveying, Thoreau wrote,

> I have offered myself much more earnestly as a lecturer than a surveyor. Yet I do not get any employment as a lecturer; was not invited to lecture once last winter, and only once (without pay) this winter. But I can get surveying enough, which a hundred others in this country can do as well as I, though it is not boasting much to say that a hundred others in New England cannot lecture as well as I on my themes.

Thoreau's surveying work didn't end when he paid his publishing debt, however. Earning fast money as a surveyor meant gaining artistic freedom as a writer. While he surveyed, he could write two million words in his journal without needing to earn a penny from them; he could pitch magazine stories that he wanted to write at the pace he wanted to write them. Contrast that to Thoreau's life in New York City, when he had to focus on writing that paid well. Back then, he even considered writing for women's lifestyle magazines—not a great fit for a man who despised consumerism—because they were among the few publications with good rates. ("They say there is a *Lady's Companion* that pays," he wrote to his mother, "but I could not write anything companionable.") Ironically, it was his work as a land surveyor that allowed Thoreau to become the first environmentalist writer. And it was when he knew to stop surveying to focus on writing that allowed Thoreau to write the masterpiece we know him for today.

The reason Thoreau became one of the most renowned writers of American literature? He knew when and how to sell out strategically. He knew when to hold 'em, when to fold 'em, when to walk away, and when to write.

Your Job Is What You Do, Not Who You Are

It was clear to Thoreau how he wanted to spend his life. He wanted to write. He wanted to have the means to support his family, too. Year by year, he found work that served these goals. Sometimes, writing was the job. Other times, surveying was the job. His goals remained consistent even as his job title changed.

It's different for most of us. We're barely in kindergarten when we're asked what we want to do when we grow up. We start with the job, and we fit a life around it. No wonder so many of us confuse what we do with who we are. Now, however, more of us wonder if we made a mistake somewhere along the way. The questioning has sparked new movements: the Great Resignation, the Big Quit, the Great Rethink. They're all different ways of saying that maybe Thoreau had it right after all. Start with life, then fit the job in.

Like Thoreau, Americans increasingly question their relationship with work. From restaurant servers to physicians to CEOs, resignation numbers show that people across career fields, income levels, and regions are asking the big question: What is it we're working for? The answer seems increasingly unclear. For almost all human history, the richer someone was, the fewer hours they worked. Logical, right? Yet that is no longer the case. Starting about twenty years ago, the richest 10 percent of married men worked the longest weeks. Why are they working so hard, if not for money?

We work to fill a spiritual void, argues journalist Derek Thompson. The less Americans rely on religion to gain meaning in their lives, the more they fill that gap with work, he wrote in the *Atlantic* story, "The Religion of Workism is Making Americans Miserable." Work has become a religious practice, in which we believe that a job is not just the means to a paycheck but also something that reveals our potential as humans: "Maybe the logic here isn't economic at all," Thompson wrote. "It's emotional—even spiritual. The best-educated and highest-earning Americans, who can have whatever they want, have chosen the office for the same reason that devout Christians attend church on Sundays: It's where they feel most themselves."

Sabbatical coach Katrina McGhee sees this in many of her clients who have a hard time stepping away from work, even temporarily, because they don't know who they'll be outside of it. "The powerful realization for a lot of these people is that work has become their identity. They might be a parent and they might be a partner, but they're sure as hell a lawyer or a top project manager because that's where they spend so much energy and time," McGhee told me. "At the end of it all, they have to disentangle that, and leaving that to take a pause is existential: 'Who am I if I'm not lawyering?' 'Who am I if I'm not project managing?'"

Psychologists call this fusion of self and job "enmeshment." Enmeshment occurs when we prioritize work so much that we grow disconnected from our own values and interests; we recognize ourselves as workers more than we do as humans. This is shaky ground on which to build an identity, however. When jobs can disappear on stakeholders' whims and promotions rely on imperfect bosses, work is a risky deity to worship. "Our desks were never meant to be our altars," Thompson wrote.

The idea that work should give our lives meaning is a fairly recent development. And, bad news, "the meaningful job" didn't begin with employers who sought to improve the quality of their workers' lives. It began as spin.

During the 1940s, when union workers negotiated pay and benefits with companies, the employer-employee arrangement was clear. Work was work; life was life. "People accepted that work was an obligation, and enjoyment was sold separately," wrote Simone Stotzoff in *The Good Enough Job: Reclaiming Life from Work*. People sought meaning and fun at home; people sought paychecks, pensions, and health care from work. That changed during the following decades as the post–World War II boom waned. When profits lagged, employers cut benefits. They reduced health care coverage, lowered retirement contributions, and axed pensions.

If employers couldn't attract workers with the lure of good benefits, they needed something else to fill that void. Enter the meaningful job. Work didn't provide the means to build a personal life; work *became* the personal life. You didn't just come to work for a paycheck, companies argued; you came to become more fully you. Or, more simply, employers cut benefits and found a way for workers to thank them for it. "In the second half of the twentieth century," Stotzoff wrote, "flexibility, individualism, and meaning supplanted job security, workplace protections, and collective solidarity for many American workers." It wasn't a good trade for everyone. Individualism and meaning can change a life, but so can health care and a pension.

Since then, the question "So what do you do?" has gotten confused with "So who are you, exactly?" Things have since spiraled into hustle culture, in which people even boast about work overtaking their personal lives. Just imagine the union workers of the 1940s—who lived the work-is-work, life-is-life philosophy—wandering into today's coworking spaces to see the neon signs that glorify nonstop work. "Eat. Sleep. Hustle. Repeat." "Home Sweet Office." "The Grind Never Stops." They'd think we lost our marbles.

How have things gotten this intense? Why did it take this culture half a century to question the long-term rewards of equating our identity with our title, our self-worth with our salary? It's time to take a few cues from Thoreau about work-life balance.

Thoreau's goal wasn't to avoid work, but to use work to achieve the life he wanted, that of a writer. Thoreau's goal wasn't even to become a rich or famous writer. He defined success by the doing, not the outcome, even when it meant he had to be a writer-surveyor or a writer-handyman. Even Emerson, his mentor and occasional frenemy, chided him for this apparent lack of drive: "Thoreau wants a little ambition in his mixture. Fault of this, instead of being the head of American Engineers, he is captain of a huckleberry party."

But Thoreau was onto something. Ambition can either compel us toward self-improvement or toward self-neglect, depending on what drives it. We must remember what motivates us, and not to confuse that with what pleases our bosses or thrills the masses.

There are two types of motivations: extrinsic and intrinsic. The people pleasers among us (raises hand) understand extrinsic motivators all too well. They're the standards that others create for us. Extrinsic motivators are why we shoot for that high GPA as teenagers and that impressive job title as adults; they're why a pat on the back or a company award feels so good. It's third-party confirmation that we're doing well for ourselves.

Intrinsic motivation, on the other hand, lies within us. It allows us to chase our curiosities. Intrinsic motivation compels us to learn and do things, simply because we find them fascinating and worthwhile; intrinsic motivation means that it's enough if the only pat we get on the back is our own. Even as we change jobs—or even if we work a job that isn't "the meaningful job"—we maintain a sense of self and success by staying attuned to intrinsic motivators. We achieve success in the pursuit more than in the recognition.

The world requires both. Extrinsic motivators are how we score raises and promotions; learning to play by others' rules is a valuable (and profitable) skill for members of a society. But take this to the extreme, and we risk falling into a black hole of organization charts and year-end reviews. We risk enmeshment. Prioritizing extrinsic motivators at the cost of intrinsic motivators can result in an eventual bewilderment over what, exactly, we're doing with our lives and who we even are. Like us, Thoreau wondered, *What do I need a job to give me? What—and who—am I working for, exactly?*

We're All Seasonal Workers Now

Thoreau believed in living life in seasons. He wrote in seasons, too. Thoreau spent two years, two months, and two days living at Walden Pond, but he condensed that time into just four seasons in *Walden*. The story of *Walden* becomes the story of seasons, and the story of a life. "There is a season for everything," Thoreau journaled. "A wise man will know what game to play to-day, and play it."

During Thoreau's seasons as a professional writer, he took low-paying editorial work that allowed him to work with other transcendentalist writers, he gave public lectures that became precursors to his most famous essays, and he supplemented those meager earnings with gig work. He barely scraped by, but "in this case my pains were their own reward," he wrote. Professional surveying, however, was Thoreau's money-making season. He did the work to pay his bills, and then he got back to the business of life. He never confused surveying with his dream job, nor did he convince himself it was anything other than a means for money. He knew what game to play each day, and he obeyed the needs of each season.

Today, jobs are catching up to the philosophy of Thoreau. The traditional career—the unwavering, linear, all-things-at-all-times career—is dying at last. People live longer today, which means we work longer, too. Half of today's five-year-olds will live to be one hundred, according to a study by the Stanford Center on Longevity, and many of these centenarians will have sixty-year careers. The center concluded that our idea of work will change as our life spans grow. The more people live to one hundred, "we won't work as we do now, cramming forty-hour weeks and fifty work weeks a year (for those who can afford to take vacation) into lives impossibly packed from morning until night with parenting, family, caregiving, schooling, and other obligations."

As we enter this next model of work, we'll think differently about how and why we work during different stages of our lives. Will we work for money or work for meaning? For most of us, it'll be a little of both, each in their own time. We'll work according to season. The principle of Waldenomics—that a price of a thing is the amount of life that's required to exchange for it—applies to jobs, too. The goal is to find a job that pays us more than it costs us, and the math behind that calculation changes as our priorities do. The value of a job without overtime skyrockets when there are kids to pick up from childcare or a passion project to complete. The value of a job with decent pay means everything to someone struggling to escape debt or saving for a home. The value of a job that provides purpose and joy offers a much-needed respite to someone who had to prioritize money for decades.

Each season has its challenges and advantages, and it's wise to adjust our work and expectations to each. There's a season to earn the money we need—and when we do, to not beat ourselves up about not having the dream gig. Hopefully, there's a season to work in a job we enjoy— and when we do, to not stress about where we fall on the organization chart or income bracket. The rare person has it all at the same time (and, let's be honest, it'd be hard to like that person very much). The key is to be honest about which season we're in. Is this meaningful-job season? Then put in those extra hours and truly care. Is this bring-home-a-paycheck season? Do the job well but prioritize the real motivations that compel your work. In Thoreau terms, we need to know which season we're in so that we know what we're willing to sacrifice for a job and what we're working to gain from it, to know "what game to play to-day, and play it."

THE GOAL: "HOW NOT TO HAVE A CAREER"

We feel the call of a new work season when we experience a workquake, according to Bruce Feiler's book, *The Search: Finding Meaningful Work in a Post-Career World*. Feiler interviewed nearly four hundred people—across genders, races, industries, and locations—about their work histories. He learned that most people have at least twenty job transitions, or workquakes. A workquake is an interruption that causes a shift in our professional lives. Workquakes are more common than we think. Some begin at the job: a lay-off, a promotion. Some begin with family: a baby, an empty nest. And others begin with health: a diagnosis, a recovery. Feiler found that the ability to navigate workquakes and adjust one's career accordingly were the keys to professional and personal success. "The very idea that our identity is based on committing to a field of work at some point and sticking with that work for decades has been irreversibly eroded," he wrote. "The most valuable skill today is no longer how to have a career. It's how not to have a career."

A workquake is a type of liminal state, the overlapping, in-between area between one phase of life and another. Thoreau loved liminal states. He found opportunity in that lost feeling between two seasons, that recognition that one era was ending and another one about to begin—even if he didn't know exactly where it would lead. Thoreau knew that those disorienting moments are when we are most likely to find ourselves because those are the moments when we're most introspective and open. "Not till we are lost, in other words, not till we have lost the world, do we begin to find ourselves, and realize where we are," he wrote.

Those liminal spaces may feel like crises but they point us to opportunities if we embrace them honestly. Think of the most beautiful times of year: They occur in the liminal spaces between seasons, with a crocus emerging from snow or the first red leaf of fall. Unfortunately, the signs of a new work season aren't always so obvious, and it's unclear sometimes when a workquake is worth the aftershocks. Then comes another uncertainty: what to do, post workquake. It's helpful to realize that the version of ourselves who chose our job might not be the same version we are today. What did that version of ourselves prioritize, and what didn't they consider?

Kathy Caprino is a career and leadership coach in Stamford, Connecticut, who's worked with thousands of clients, mostly midcareer women who've achieved professional success but seek something beyond it. Caprino shared that even among high-earning, high-performing workers, the reasons behind their career choices can be arbitrary and even subconscious. One client, for example, decided at the age of twelve that she'd go into sales. The reason for her choice? This woman grew up with an alcoholic, unstable parent, and when she was twelve, she saw a television character who was a successful saleswoman. As a kid, she believed that going into sales would mean that she could always take care of herself as an adult. And she did just that. Years later, after this woman advanced in her field and achieved financial success, she came to Caprino in crisis. The woman, who had achieved more success than most people could dream of, felt "broken." A frightened child had set her path, and she grew into an unquestioning adult who feared to leave it behind.

Although that story may seem extreme, it's not unusual. Most of us chose careers at young ages and for somewhat unrealistic reasons. We'd never stick with a hairstyle that our sixteen-year-old self had chosen. We'd never stay loyal to a plan hatched in college, especially one based on which majors didn't have Friday classes. But, somehow, we follow career paths set by a version of ourselves who wasn't old enough to rent a car—and when we don't deviate from those plans, it's easy to mistake our fear of change for steadfastness.

Most of us don't have the luxury to decide whether to work, but we get to choose how to work. The choice begins with two questions: What do we need from our jobs, and what are we willing to give them? There's no right answer to those questions, and any answer will likely change throughout our life, creating many chances to self-correct. Just ask Henry David Thoreau, the writer-editor-surveyor-handyman–manure shoveler.

"Writing is like driving at night in the fog," wrote E. L. Doctorow. "You can only see as far as your headlights, but you can make the whole trip that way." Thoreau's life proves that a career can be the same way, as long as we're wise enough to recognize a well-timed exit.

The Perks of Being a Quitter

If you happened to be in Brooklyn's Prospect Park in the winter of 2019, you might've seen a guy sitting on a park bench with four leashed dogs at his feet. His eyes were closed, his face was lifted to the sun, and a smile was plastered across his face. If you were close enough, you'd hear him say, "Worth it. Soooo worth it."

That guy, Michael Josephs, recently quit his job. He'd been a special education teacher, and although he enjoyed his work with students, he didn't enjoy the lifestyle that came with his schedule and commute. In the winter, for example, he left for work before sunrise, came home after sunset, and never saw the sun. For an outdoorsy person, remaining inside year-round and missing sunlight for a quarter of the year came at too high a cost. Josephs wanted a career that would give him "fresh breath of air moments." Josephs thought about when he was happiest: Often, it was when he was walking and training his rescue dog Willy at the park. Passersby would stop what they were doing to watch these training sessions; Josephs not only had a natural talent for dog training, but he took great enjoyment in it, too. It gave him an idea.

When Josephs told his colleagues that he was quitting his job to open a dog-walking business, they gave him all the what-ifs: What if he failed? What if he squandered years of teaching experience to start over in a job with more risk than certainty? His wife, however, saw his enthusiasm and energy and responded another way: Let's do this.

The first year Josephs ran Parkside Pups, he didn't earn much money. But the first time he sat down on a Prospect Park bench midday and enjoyed the winter sun—his "fresh breath of air moment"—he knew: It was worth it. Soooo worth it. The job let him tap into a new part of his brain, and he discovered how much he enjoyed (and excelled at) launching a brand. Now, five years later, Josephs has eleven team members at Parkside Pups, with services offered in Brooklyn, the Financial District, and Battery Park. He's added boarding and training services, and he's considering grooming services as well. Even with a staff, Josephs still walks clients' dogs, including on "Willy Wednesdays" when his own pup joins the packs. Josephs earns more than he did as a teacher, but even better, he has a job that gives him the life he wanted.

"I enjoy time with the dogs, time I get to spend as their second special person," Josephs told me. "And I set my schedule, so I get time to focus on my family, take bigger hikes with Willy, go mountain biking, and whatever I need to be able to be happy. It's priceless."

It was only when Josephs defined what he was working to gain—more time outdoors, more availability for his family—that he could choose the work that was right for him. But he couldn't start his new venture without doing the thing most of us hate to do: quit.

It's time to stop equating quitting with failure, wrote Julia Keller in *Quitting: A Life Strategy*. Quitting can get easier with time, and it can make us more flexible and adventurous: "The good news is that the more times you ask your brain to do something it's never done before, to try something new—that is to go in another direction after it has quit the present one—the better it gets at doing that. An active brain is a happy brain. Quitting is like aerobics for your brain."

For Michael Josephs, quitting his teaching career to start a dog-walking business brought him the victory he sought: a job that gave him "fresh breath-of-air moments." But it scored him another victory he didn't anticipate: realizing that he was capable of starting a new venture, of building something from scratch. He gained the confidence to take bigger risks. Once Josephs knew he could start a business, he tried more things with less fear. It's why, since then, he's begun a side venture in real estate, investing profits from his dog-walking company into a new endeavor. Quitting was his first step in gaining momentum and confidence throughout his life.

"I can take the skills and the experiences that I've had from the last five years, and I can build a different venture," Josephs told me. "I think that's been the biggest factor: I have options. Before I started this company, I felt like I didn't have any options."

Enmeshment is poison to the idea of quitting and beginning anew. If Thoreau had enmeshed as a teacher— "Who am I if not a teacher?"—we'd never have known him as a great writer. If Josephs had enmeshed as a teacher, he'd never have known himself to be a successful entrepreneur and investor.

Quitting a job isn't the only way to create a new start, however. Quitting a mind-set can be powerful, too. After all, the job might not be the problem; we might be. New seasons can begin with new boundaries. For example, Caprino counseled a woman who enjoyed her job but felt burned out by 2:00 a.m. emails and constant online connection to work. Yet these problems didn't result from corporate policy; they emerged from a behavior that Caprino has seen in thousands of women, what she calls "perfectionistic over-functioning." "It's doing more than is healthy, appropriate, and trying to get that A+," Caprino explained. "If you don't address and overcome this debilitating behavior, you'll constantly chase a target that's never achievable. You'll most likely end up feeling sick and burned out."

Instead of guiding her client to a new career, Caprino encouraged this woman to establish new boundaries in her current one, to shift away from the mind-set of perfectionistic over-functioning. The woman established rules for herself and her department about off-hours availability, and her entire team benefitted. When she changed what she worked for—no longer working for that A+ but instead instilling a culture of balance—she not only enjoyed her job more but developed as a leader. "It worked beautifully,"

Caprino said. The woman didn't enter a new season with a new career, but a fresh perspective.

Another example of finding a new season through boundaries comes from one of my professional inspirations, Kat Boogaard. She's a tremendously successful freelance writer, based out of Appleton, Wisconsin, whose business brought in nearly $300,000 of revenue in 2021. That year, she had her second son, and the old thrill she felt from running a successful business became overshadowed by the burnout of life as a working parent. The solution wasn't to quit; Boogaard realized that a new life season called for a new business plan.

"I want to combat hustle culture, but the reality is that I still need to earn money. I have a family and need to pay for childcare," Boogaard told me. "Combatting hustle culture would be a lot easier if we could all just be like, 'Well, screw work!' You have to live somewhere in the gray."

Boogaard realized she'd been so focused on making as much money as possible that she didn't know how much money she'd need to make to maintain her family's standard of living. She needed boundaries to define her new shade of gray. "If it's up to me, I'll just keep moving the finish line," she admitted.

After she and her husband crunched numbers, Boogaard created a monthly income cap—not a goal, but a cap. Once she hit that cap, Boogaard could choose to take projects she'd enjoy, but she wouldn't accept work out of a scarcity mind-set. (Look at the budgeting lists in *Walden*, and you'll see that Thoreau used the same strategy.)

Boogaard discovered she could downshift to a four-day workweek and still hit her cap. Soon after, she could do it in just three days a week. To do so, she simplified her business: She scaled back her use of subcontractors, raised her rates, reduced social media marketing, and communicated new boundaries to clients (no same-day meetings, no rush jobs). None of her clients blinked; she had years of good relationships with them and her new boundaries and rates didn't change that. While Boogaard's income decreased, she still earns what she needs from a job she loves, while enjoying the life it allows her to have beyond it.

How to Begin Again

A workquake should help us understand where we are in life, which season we need to end and which we'd like to begin. Caprino's first tip to clients who want to explore new career options is to remember what's made them stand out. She asks clients: What activities and subjects have they enjoyed and excelled at—in childhood, adolescence, adulthood? What talents have come easier to them than to others that bring joy and make them feel fully alive? These gifts and abilities point to areas of natural inclination and talent to explore. "Dwell as near as possible to the channel in which your life flows," Thoreau wrote.

I would add another question: What makes you weird? Think of Thoreau. When he thought of ways to make money, it must've occurred to him that he once surveyed Walden Pond by himself for the thrill of it (weird!). It was a uniquely Thoreau thing to do, and it pointed him toward his next move. That which makes us weird makes us special. I was a web developer who went to grad school in English just for fun (weird!), so veering to a career in writing seemed about right. Think of what made Caprino and Josephs stand out. Caprino's always been the person keenly interested in what makes people tick, and even back in high school, she was the person people sought out for advice; Josephs had a natural gift for training dogs and connecting with them. Over time, Caprino said, many people have forgotten about those things that light them up, the areas where they contribute something unique to the world. "We often forget who we really are in our dogged pursuit of money and success," she told me.

The next step is to vet our dreams, which may be trickier than it seems. Caprino has heard the bed-and-breakfast dream quite a bit in her work. Clients come to her, burned out from high-stress corporate careers, and a surprising number of them share a similar dream: "I just want to quit my job and run my own charming bed and breakfast"—the Newhart dream.

Even as adults, it's hard to dream the right dream for ourselves. Caprino calls this the "pendulum effect," when people leave one bad job but overcorrect in the opposite direction. (My plan to leave a web development job to hike the Appalachian Trail is a prime example.)

When clients come to Caprino with the B&B dream— or the novel-writing dream or the chef dream—she encourages them to vet the dream first. She'll have them research the new field and talk to people who successfully work in that field, as well as people who've decided to leave that field. How much money do they make? What do their days look like? What do they like and dislike about the work? The B&B dream looks much less dreamy when considered from the perspective of the owner and not the guest. Even Bob Newhart woke up from the Newhart dream.

If a hobby doesn't survive the career-vetting process, it still may nudge you for more of your time. Caprino told me that the happiest people she meets are those who have a mosaic life. "They've forged a beautiful mix of what they do for a living that bring rewards and satisfaction, and also exciting endeavors that bring them meaning, purpose, and joy outside of what they do for a living."

Find a job that can be part of a mosaic throughout your seasons. Josephs's job allows him to go mountain biking. Caprino's job allows her to travel, sing, and play tennis. Mine lets me garden in the middle of the day. Thoreau's surveying work allowed him to take long walks through the woods. When life is a mosaic, people can add tiles that create something beautiful together. They can enjoy work without enmeshing with it. It's something that Boogaard discovered, too, after she created boundaries at work.

"I have so many other things that are meaningful to me, that provide purpose and fulfillment and growth, outside of the way I earn my money," Boogaard said. "My career used to be my identity, how I defined myself. It's gone from being the whole pie to just a slice." Or, perhaps, just one sparkly tile in her mosaic.

Five Questions: Rethinking Work

1. If you could have any job without worry- ing about money—even a job that might not exist yet—what would it be? Think about what you would enjoy about working that job, why your traits or skills would align with it, and what oppor- tunities it would give you.

2. How would you rank the following things in terms of importance to you at work?

   - The type of work you do
   - The coworkers you have
   - The setting where you work
   - The financial compensation
   - The level of prestige

3. If you needed to make a high income as quickly as possible, which job would you do? (Keep it legal, people.) Think about how this job would play to your strengths, as well as how long you'd be able to do this job without burning out.

4. After Thoreau spent time living in Emerson's cushy house, he wrote that he must "beware a dangerous prosperity"—in other words, to resist the golden handcuffs that could trap him at a job long past its season. If you intended to take a short-term, lucrative job, how could you set yourself up to escape the golden handcuffs when it was time to leave?

5. Think of your life in seasons and think of the demands and opportunities of each season (e.g., single life, childrearing, college debt repayment, semi-retirement). What jobs would you choose today for each season?

Spend Life Lavishly

*The point of simplifying isn't
to have less. It's to make room
for what matters more.*

*When he has obtained those things which are necessary
to life, there is another alternative
than to obtain the superfluities:
and that is, to adventure on life now.*
—HENRY DAVID THOREAU

*The ability to simplify means to eliminate the
unnecessary so that the necessary may speak.*
—HANS HOFMAN

So much of Thoreau's writing focuses on simplification that it can be easy to miss his point: What did Thoreau simplify for? His end goal wasn't to do and to have less, but to clear space and time for what truly mattered. This is the fun part of Waldenomics: spending life lavishly, reaping that profit.

Let's turn to the priorities that inspired Thoreau to spend his time, his energy, his money—his life—in ways that paid him back, which can inspire us to think how we might do so, too.

THOREAU, FAMILY MAN AND GOOD NEIGHBOR

By now, we know how much Thoreau supported his family, practically, emotionally, and financially. His ideas revolutionized his father's pencil factory and produced the country's finest pencil, lifting the Thoreau family into comfortable middle-class life. He contributed to the down payment on the family home that his mother ran as a boarding house, and he even dug its cellar out himself. When John, Thoreau's brother and closest friend, contracted tetanus at twenty-seven after he nicked his finger with a razor, Thoreau cared for him. John died in his arms.

Thoreau was a devoted family man. The letters he wrote to his mom about his work struggles in New York City show how close the two were. While he was at Walden Pond, his family visited him at the cabin each Saturday, and he continued to go home for Sunday night dinners. Critics allege these family visits are signs of Thoreau's hypocrisy, even if he never claimed to spend those years in solitude. (Thoreau devoted an entire chapter in *Walden* to "Visitors." He wasn't trying to get away with anything here. In the chapter, he recalls how he could fit about thirty people into his cabin at once.)

In his excellent book, *The Thoreau You Don't Know: What the Prophet of Environmentalism Really Meant*, Robert Sullivan paints a picture of Thoreau unlike any I've read before. When Thoreau lived at home and his mother booked boarding guests, she would enlist her son to help entertain them:

> A visitor calls and Henry David is called for. Eventually, he comes racing down the stairs. He's dancing, a short-legged, slope-shouldered lanky bachelor in his late thirties. . . . He is dancing a jig, his feet shuffling, kicking, a burst of joy. . . . "My Henry always was a good dancer," his mother will tell the visitors.

When I picture this scene of mega-introvert Thoreau running down the stairs to dance in the living room to help his mother entertain her boarding guests, I think, this is a man who really loved his mom.

Despite his introversion, Thoreau prioritized time with neighbors and friends as well. He was famous for his annual melon party. He'd spend the summer growing melons—known as the best in town—and during the late summer, he'd set up long tables and invite the town to share in his harvest. He continued to host his melon parties while he lived at Walden Pond.

Too many people believe Thoreau was an antisocial writer who went to the woods to turn his back on society. But consider how intentionally he lived his life at Walden Pond and how he omitted any unnecessary thing that didn't add value to his experience there. Then consider that even during the scarcity of his Walden experiment, he believed that family dinners and his annual melon party were among life's most essential things. When he brought just twenty-four items to the cabin, three of them were chairs that he offered to visitors. After his various living arrangements—in New York, at the pond, in Emerson's home—Thoreau spent the rest of his life in an attic room of the house where he felt most comfortable: his family's home, ready at a moment's notice to head downstairs, dancing.

THOREAU AS NATURE LOVER

Thoreau believed that any day was wasted when he couldn't spend four hours walking in nature. Four hours! Even during the hottest afternoons of summer and the snowiest days of a Massachusetts winter, Thoreau wanted to spend as much time as possible outdoors. "It is true, I never assisted the sun materially in its rising, but, doubt not, it was of the last importance only to be present at it," he wrote.

Walden is full of moments of Thoreau being fully present in nature, finding wonder and beauty in ordinary moments. For example, the book has a section about two kinds of ants, red ants and black ants, engaged in a battle to the death. Thoreau sets the scene with plenty of detail and ant drama. ("They fought with more pertinacity than bull-dogs. Neither manifested the least disposition to retreat.") The ant battle section goes on for nearly 1,200 words! You'd be forgiven for getting a tad bored during this section. But it makes me smile, just wondering how long Thoreau sat there watching those ants, then finding them worthy of taking up 1,200 words in a book about minimalism. This moment, one that most of us wouldn't have even noticed, became a fascinating source of study, simply because he paid attention to the wonder that surrounds us, if only we notice.

Readers complain of the drudgery of *Walden*'s middle chapters. Perhaps. The book is front- and back-loaded with those great quotes we associate with Thoreau ("The mass of men lead lives of quiet desperation"), and it concludes with some of those passages we love most ("If you have built castles in the air, your work need not be lost; that is where they should be. Now put the foundations under them"). But the middle chapters? An ant battle. A frozen pond. Beans. It slows down, but that is the point. Thoreau makes his reader pause with him to notice the small details and to luxuriate in the quiet. It reminds me of a great vacation: During the first couple days, I cram as much fun in as possible (I love an itinerary), but a few days later, the trip teaches me to slow down, to find contentment in a sunrise, to realize that feeling the warmth of sun on my face is pleasure enough. Think of *Walden* like a great vacation, one that teaches you to slow down and look around a bit. Maybe even watch ants for a while.

Not many readers do this, however. The next time you're in a used bookstore, page through a copy of *Walden*. I bet that the first pages will be underlined and dog-eared, and the spine over the middle pages will never have been cracked open. This breaks my heart. I beg you to stick with those middle chapters. Slow your mind. Find magic in a freezing pond, company in the hoots of owls. These moments, above all, were what Thoreau lived for. And when I'm able to calm my scattered mind enough to do this, I realize how wise he was to prioritize these quiet moments in nature, simply paying attention.

THOREAU, THE ACTIVIST

Let's think back on Thoreau as the adorable tightwad he was. He built his cabin with $28 worth of materials. Walden has list after list of things he needed and how cheaply he could get them, down to the half-penny (seriously). He hated needing money because he hated earning it. I can't blame him.

Then consider this. In 1850, the Fugitive Slave Act made it a crime for northerners to help enslaved people escape. In fact, it required northerners to assist in slaves' recapture, making Yankees complicit in system of slavery. Anyone who did not comply with this law could be fined $1,000 and get six months in jail. By this time, Thoreau and his family were outspoken abolitionists. Frederick Douglass even stayed at the Thoreau family home, and Douglass became friends with Thoreau's sister, Helen. The entire Thoreau family were long-time operatives of the Underground Railroad, giving escaped slaves a safe space to stay and helping them with their safe passage to Canada. What would this law mean for their work?

Think of it: $1,000. That's about four years of salary for Thoreau, and twice the down payment on the family home. So what did the Thoreaus do after this law passed? Thoreau and his family continued to serve as operatives on the Underground Railroad. Formerly enslaved people found sanctuary at the Thoreau family home, then at night, Thoreau would escort them to the nearby West Fitchburg rail station—scouting the way beforehand to ensure that authorities weren't present. With each enslaved person they helped, the Thoreau family risked bankruptcy and prison. Yet they feared a worse punishment. Thoreau, his parents, and his sisters recognized the moral bankruptcy that would come if they didn't continue to fight for justice and oppose slavery, no matter the risk.

It's a tough question, though: Would you risk four years' salary to take a moral stand? The next time you hear someone rant that Thoreau was morally compromised because of his laundry habits, consider that this was a man with a sense of purpose so strong that he didn't hesitate answering yes to that question.

During his forties, Thoreau took his antislavery activism further. John Brown was the radical abolitionist who advocated for violent rebellion against slaveholders, even their murder if necessary. Much to his neighbors' disapproval, Thoreau supported Brown publicly. At the hour of Brown's execution, Thoreau planned to deliver a speech in Concord to memorialize him, and about five hundred people threatened to counter-demonstrate—with guns. Thoreau gave his John Brown speech, undeterred. He later had the speech published to widen its audience. Thoreau, whom we associate with civil disobedience and peaceful protest, said that in the case of slavery, violence might be the only answer to overcome it. In his speech for Brown, he said, "I do not wish to kill nor to be killed, but I can foresee circumstances in which both these things would be by me unavoidable." It's a side of Thoreau often underappreciated by his critics: Thoreau, ethical badass.

Spend Big, Round Hours

Each daunting statistic in this book has a positive counterpoint. If the average American spends four and a half hours a day on their phone, totaling two months of scrolling per year, cutting that time in half can give us a month of our life back. Imagine gaining one month of found time! If most people wear 20 percent of their clothes 80 percent of the time, reducing those unnecessary purchases gives us lots of cash to spend on more useful things. If most creative geniuses reveal feeling "odd" or "different" from their peers, what could we achieve if we too accepted our quirks as our superpowers?

It's time to spend your Waldenomics profit. Now that we've learned to streamline our stuff and our schedule, create a little space from the world, embrace our inner misfit, and work seasonally, how do we use our time? Our money? Our energy? We've pared down; now we trade up.

Thoreau's life offers the right inspiration to get started. Thoreau created a life philosophy that began with values, not goals. Remember what we learned from Dr. Lakshmin in the retreat chapter. Values are who we are, goals are what we do. Thoreau lived a life that prioritized values: his connections with people, his love of nature, and his devotion to individual freedom. He placed his goals—whether for work, finances, or daily habits—in service to those values.

Most of us do the opposite. We start with goals, thinking they'll eventually accumulate into values. It's an understandable strategy when we live in a time of such hustle and change that it's hard to see past the current day. To focus on our next step seems like a reasonable strategy. The problem is when we become so focused on the goals in front of us that we neglect the values beyond them. We focus on what we do, not who we are. And then eventually, we become unsure who we really are at all.

I write this not as a teacher but as a fellow seeker in the values-over-goals quest. I spent many years striving to be the ideal employee, praised by bosses and colleagues for my willingness to go the extra mile. (When Caprino used the term "perfectionistic over-functioning" in our conversation, I groaned in recognition.) But then I'd complain about not having time for my real life: my husband, my friends, travel, my stack of to-read books. My biggest regret has been the extra hours I've given to bosses I didn't even like that I could've spent with people and hobbies I loved. My immediate goals obscured my big-picture values.

"If I repent of anything, it is very likely to be my good behaviour," Thoreau wrote. "What demon possessed me that I behaved so well?" Ditto, Henry.

Aligning time with values requires work and intention, and the person who's helped me do this better—next to Thoreau—is writer Anne Lamott, who gave me the phrase that reminds me to spend time well. It comes from a line in *Bird by Bird* about her best friend with cancer. "Time is so full for people who are dying in a conscious way, full in the way that life is for children," Lamott wrote. "They spend big round hours." Thoreau, due to tuberculosis, knew he wouldn't have a long life. The awareness likely inspired him to spend big round hours. But big round hours don't tug at our sleeves, asking for our time like our bosses do; big round hours don't ping us with notifications on our phones. They wait for us to slow down enough to discover them. Those middle chapters of *Walden*? Big round hours.

All of us, if we're wise, know that we're counting down our four thousand weeks. So how do we spend our time in a way that aligns with our values? How do we spend more big round hours that reflect the people we really are and the things that really matter to us?

Simplifying can be key in identifying our values. By removing everything that's unnecessary, we can enjoy the essential.

If paring down to trade up sounds like too much of a sacrifice, Joshua Becker offers another angle to consider. All of us are minimalists already. Right now. "Everyone is minimizing something," Becker wrote in *Things That Matter*. "If you're not minimizing your possessions, you're minimizing your money, time, and potential." Or, perhaps, you're minimizing your big round hours.

THE UNHAPPY SIDE OF HAPPINESS

Each year, one of the most common New Year's resolutions is to be happy. As a goal, this one's a stinker. It's understandable, sure. Who doesn't want to be happy? But no one can be happy all the time, and much less so when we pressure ourselves into an impossible good-vibes-only mode. "And I get it: I want to be happy, too," wrote Catherine Price in *The Power of Fun: How to Feel Alive Again*. "But announcing that we'd like to 'be happy' is about as practical as announcing that we'd like to be taller."

Creating a happy life involves, unfortunately, a little misery. Arthur C. Brooks, who teaches courses on happiness and leadership at Harvard Business School, defines three "macronutrients" of happiness: enjoyment, satisfaction, and purpose. Ironically, they all require unhappiness: "Enjoyment takes work and forgoing pleasures; satisfaction requires sacrifice and doesn't last; purpose almost always entails suffering."[1] This was true for Thoreau. The enjoyment he got from his family required him to put aside his writing to help them, the satisfaction of his environmental research involved walks in the rain and snow, and the purpose of abolitionism resulted in death threats.

The question is whether all that sacrifice was worth it. After all, Thoreau was criticized and mocked for living a life that looked different from his neighbors, only to become a writer who died without much fame. Yet, I believe that the proof that he lived well lies in the details of his death. In a letter from Thoreau in March 1862, two months before his death, he wrote that he knew he would die soon, but he was "enjoying existence as much as ever, and regret[s] nothing." Later, after his friend Sam Staples visited Thoreau on his deathbed, Staples wrote of the encounter, "Never saw a man dying with so much pleasure & peace."

Achieving a good life through intentional choices is an idea echoed by Becker: "How we get to the end of our lives with minimal regrets: We choose well," he wrote. "We set aside lesser pursuits to seek meaning in our lives. And we do it every single day."

Thoreau put aside lesser pursuits to seek meaning through time with family and neighbors, enjoyment of nature, and dedication to justice—connection, hobbies, purpose. It's a trifecta that we could do well to emulate.

Above All, People

I learn from Thoreau the most when he seemed to act like the stereotypical Thoreau the least. What compelled this legendary loafer to put in extra hours to earn additional money? What did he find to be worth even more than his time alone holding a pen or wandering the woods? It's an easy answer. It was his family and friends.

There are times when Thoreau behaved very un-Thoreau-like, working long hours as a surveyor, traveling to New York City for meetings, and focusing on matters of business. When he did, it was usually in service to others: supporting his father's pencil factory when it faltered, helping his mom earn the down payment for her boarding home, or paying the publishing debt for the book about his boat trip with his brother. He even took over the pencil factory after his father died. It's a side of him we don't think about: Henry David Thoreau, businessman.

When it came between what Thoreau most wanted to do and what he felt called to do, the latter would win when it was a matter of his most valued relationships. This included more than just his family; think of the community-wide invitation to his melon party each year. A man who found solitude to be his closest companion threw a shindig every summer and invited the whole town to share in his harvest. We know Thoreau for his love of nature, but perhaps we should appreciate him more for his love of people, too.

Prioritizing people in our lives is the best way to lead a happy life. If you don't take it from Thoreau, take it from his alma mater, Harvard University. Researchers there showed that Thoreau's priority of people was more than kind, it was also the smartest way to live a good life. In the Harvard Study of Adult Development, researchers followed the lives of 724 men for seventy-five years to learn what most affected happiness and health throughout a lifetime. Participants included the rich and the poor (including a Harvard sophomore named John F. Kennedy). Researchers asked for updates throughout their lives: How's work? How's family? How's your health? To the researchers' surprise, the biggest predictor of a healthy, happy life was the presence of close relationships—even more than wealth, good genes, or fame.

"What are the lessons that come from the tens of thousands of pages of information that we've generated on these lives? The lessons aren't about wealth or fame or working harder and harder," said Robert Waldinger, the fourth director of the study who's a professor of psychiatry at Harvard Medical School, in a TED Talk. "The clearest message we get from this seventy-five-year study is this: Good relationships keep us happier and healthier. Period."

The study showed that the benefit of close relationships had nothing to do with the types of relationships, or even the number of relationships. It didn't matter if someone was single or married, if they had two close friends or fifty. It only mattered that they enjoyed close connections with others.

More research supports this. A report by the US Surgeon General found that loneliness harms health as much as smoking fifteen cigarettes a day. Another study showed that the more types of relationships we have—including family, friends, coworkers, and even strangers we strike up conversations with—is a unique predictor of our well-being throughout our lifetime.[2]

Yet time with others is on the decline. Historically, the amount of time people have spent with friends remained fairly stable, right around six and a half hours per week—until 2014, that is. Then that figure took a dive. In 2019, it went down to four hours per week. By 2021, it was just two hours, forty-five minutes. What changed? The percent of people with smartphones crossed the 50 percent mark in 2014.[3] We hang out more with our phones than we hang out with each other.

THE MEDICINE OF HANGING OUT

"Hanging out is about daring to do nothing much and, even more than that, daring to do it in the company of others," wrote Sheila Liming in *Hanging Out: The Radical Power of Killing Time*. This seems to be the core problem lurking behind our loneliness. Like in work, we seek a trick, a productivity hack, a whitepaper to attack this issue. Instead, the answer might be much simpler than that. It might just be prioritizing what seems impossible to prioritize: doing nothing much, and doing it more often with others.

A lot of something can come from a lot of nothing. I think of a close group of my friends, a group of eleven who came together one Sunday evening early in the pandemic to play Zoom trivia. At that time, I was good friends with a few of them, while I barely knew most. One of them has since laughingly admitted that she logged onto that first trivia night begrudgingly, but hey, social options were sparse in March of 2020. The next Sunday, we all logged on again. Same for the next. Each week, our games got goofier and longer. We started theme nights, awarding extra credit for costumes, assembled by whatever we found in our closets and attics. Drinks and conversations lasted hours after the winner was announced, and we learned more about each other and our families. Post-COVID, we gathered in person, at breweries or wine gardens where the kids could run around while the adults sat around talking about nothing much. We now celebrate birthdays and holidays together. A remarkably close relationship formed between eleven people simply because we dared to do nothing much together, and we did it often.

As I write this, I'm recovering from emergency lung surgery. The last couple weeks have been among the scariest and most painful I've had. On my second day in the hospital, an enormous bouquet of flowers arrived at my bedside, signed "The Trivia Crew." They sent me adorable video messages from their kids wishing me well, and they texted photos of their pets to cheer me up. When my husband stayed with me at the hospital, they walked our dogs. When I got home, they dropped off meals and my favorite snacks. (I can attest to the healing powers of Cheez-Its and Peanut M&Ms.) They checked in on me while I dealt with the isolation and pain of recovery, and they sent me names of the best specialists in the state. During a time of crisis, these friends were my lifeline. Out of so much nothing came absolutely everything.

I wonder if this may be why so many of our close adult friendships began in college dorms. A group of strangers comes together in one hall, and that's where they spend so much time doing nothing together: killing hours between classes, getting ready for parties, nursing hangovers and heartbreaks. Those times didn't look like anything much at the time, but now, looking back, they were everything. (Thoreau wrote that the most valuable part of higher education is the only part that colleges don't charge for: the friendships that students make with each other.)

The more contrived and forced versions of relationship building in the adult world—think of networking events or the dreaded icebreaker activities—rarely do the trick. Intimacy comes from much more ordinary stuff. It comes from something as simple as a weekly trivia game or an annual melon party. It comes from just taking the time (as Liming so beautifully put it) daring to do nothing much in the company of others.

Remember Kat Boogaard, the writer who adopted a three-day workweek? I asked her how her life had changed with her new schedule. She laughed and apologized for not having a "glamorous" answer for me. Yet the joy in her voice spoke volumes as she described an average week. Each week, her family celebrates the sacred tradition of Taco Tuesday for dinner. On Friday mornings, she and her boys run errands together, going to Target, to the library, to a playground and then grocery shopping (choosing the cart with the race car steering wheels). She and her husband have more date nights, and she has time to meet girlfriends for pedicures.

"It's just been more time and energy to enjoy the simple pleasures," Boogaard told me. "We really need that balance, those interactions. We were not meant to be alone in front of a screen for twelve hours a day, six days a week. It's no way to live."

I think about how much Boogaard sacrificed and strategized to achieve her new schedule. What made it worthwhile for her to take a serious hit in income was the opportunity to simply spend time with the people she loves, doing nothing much together.

"We must wrest time away from the places where it has been sequestered and kept from us against our will," wrote Liming. "We must work to seize and redistribute the wealth that is time and, when we have done that, we must commit to the work of giving it all back to each other."

Prioritize a Hobby Like It's Your Job

Rod Stewart has an elaborate model train. Julia Roberts is a knitter. Brad Pitt makes pottery. Mike Tyson, I kid you not, races pigeons.

As for Thoreau? "For many years I was self-appointed inspector of snow-storms and rain-storms, and did my duty faithfully; surveyor, if not of highways, then of forest paths and all across-lot routes, keeping them open, and ravines bridged and passable at all seasons, where the public heel had testified to their utility."

In other words, Thoreau was a walker. No matter the weather, he wanted to be outside, walking in fresh air and studying nature. Neighbors would watch him walk out of town into the woods and return, hours later, carrying samples of plants and flowers perched on the brim of his hat for later study. Many of them thought he was a total weirdo. He didn't care. He loved his nature walks. "It is a great art to saunter," he journaled.

This was about more than sauntering, however. Thoreau scholar Brent Ranalli said that one underappreciated aspect of Thoreau are contributions as a scientist. Later in his life, he corresponded with academic scientists and made his own discoveries that he recorded in his journal. "Thoreau was doing the science that he wanted to do, at the pace he wanted to do it, pursuing the questions that he wanted to pursue," Ranalli told me. "He was not concerned about what other people thought were interesting questions or what kind of reactions he would get from his work." Thoreau studied nature simply because he found it fun and fascinating. He might be tickled to learn how many climate scientists use his journal in their research today and how many of his entries have become crucial data points in environmental studies.

Thoreau was onto something with all his nature walks and studies. While neighbors just saw a guy taking yet another walk into the woods, scientists today would see a person who prioritized hobbies, and with them, his physical and mental health. People who engage in hobbies on a regular basis can lower their blood pressure and reduce their body mass index.[4] Hobbies can even decrease one's risk for dementia.[5] If there was a pill for that, we'd take it. But, here, the medicine might look more like a pottery class or an afternoon of bird watching. It's yet more evidence that being a more well-rounded human makes us a healthier human, too.

Embracing fun and hobbies is on the rise even in the productivity-obsessed United States. People spend more time doing non-work-related things like gardening, reading, and cooking—about six hours a week. In 2023, a Gallup poll showed a 13 percent increase in the number of adults who believe that hobbies and recreational activities are extremely or very important.[6]

It sounds easy and obvious, right? Having fun is, well, fun. But having fun, ironically, is hard, especially now. It involves intention and choice and focus. For most of us, fun necessitates putting down our phones long enough to find it. After all, spending more than four hours a day on our phone is rarely our intention. We pick them up to check the weather, and then somehow, it's several hours later and we've watched funny dog videos, bookmarked recipes that we'll never make, and learned what happened to that kid in eighth grade whom we only just remembered we forgot.

In *The Power of Fun*, Price calls such distractions—especially our phone distractions—"fake fun." We slip into these activities unintentionally, thinking they'll be enjoyable enough, but after a while, they leave us feeling unsatisfied. Price compares fake fun to junk food. If you snack on a cheesy poof or two, it's delightful. If you eat the whole bag, you feel gross.

Why do we settle for filling our precious free time with so much fake fun? Number one, it's easier to pick up what's in front of us, which will often be our phone. And number two, plenty of companies make fortunes tempting us to engage in fake fun. "If we don't know what True Fun looks or feels like . . . then we will be left with empty space and no idea how we want to fill it," Price wrote. "The companies behind our most time-sucking apps have an economic incentive to take advantage of this vacuum and suck up our energy and attention, leaving us too exhausted to do anything else."

Having true fun involves real work. It makes us ask not only what fun is, but it makes us wonder who we really are.

What do we enjoy? What energizes us? What leaves us feeling as though we're tapping into something special within us, while connecting with something worthwhile beyond us? Only then will we be prepared to make an upgrade: trade fake fun for true fun. If the average American cut their phone time in half, they could gain two hours of true fun *every day*. Imagine what that could mean to the quality of a day, of a life.

Price acknowledges that analyzing fun might not be, well, fun, but it's an essential first step. To begin, she defines the three elements of "true fun": (1) playfulness, doing something for the simple enjoyment of it, and not for a specified outcome; (2) connection, a shared experience with a person or thing; and (3) flow, the timeless state that occurs when we're absorbed in an activity. Anything can be play, and it's less about the activity we do and more about the attitude that we bring to it. We can have true fun while playing pickleball, baking a cake, or (in the case of our buddy Thoreau) taking a stroll through the woods to see what's blooming today.

The more time we invest in fun, the more fun it'll be. In *Digital Minimalism*, Cal Newport teaches the Bennett principle: "the value you receive from a pursuit is often proportional to the energy invested." We need to get serious about fun, in other words, to maximize our Waldenomics profit.

My friend Scott Greenberg is a case study in fun and the Bennett principle. Greenberg loves music more than anyone I know. As a teenager in Detroit, he dreamed of a career in radio. After getting his first radio gig after college, Greenberg realized that it wasn't a job in radio he was after. He simply wanted a life surrounded by music. "What I really wanted to do was to play the music I wanted to hear, and I wanted to talk too much about it," he said with a laugh. "I was just a big music nerd."

Greenberg created a new life strategy. Just as Thoreau kept his scientific research as his hobby and not his job, Greenberg chose to make music his personal project and not his career. He left his radio job to become a corporate marketing writer—regular hours, better pay—but he remained pure music nerd. For the past twenty-two years, Greenberg has hosted a radio show called *Debts No Honest Man Can Pay*. (Coincidentally, my book begins, and nearly ends, with Bruce Springsteen references.) His goal for his show is joy; this isn't a side hustle tied to a professional objective. To hear *Debts* is to hear someone having true fun. But his true fun continues off the air. His life has become research for the show. He's always at concerts, from tiny stages at dive bars to major festivals with big acts, and he listens to new releases from obscure and well-known bands. He invites other music lovers to join him on his show as guests, and they talk too much about music together. How much does Greenberg get paid for his show? Nothing. Has he achieved massive fame or a cult following? Not really. When he hosted *Debts* on internet radio a decade ago, metrics revealed that sometimes only a handful of people tuned into a show that took him hours to put together. So why does Greenberg do it, week after week? Because the work of his show has been an essential part of his fun.

"I've gained a sense of craft. Of accomplishment," he said. The show, which is now a podcast, inspires him to live a life that prioritizes music. It's introduced him to fellow music lovers, and he's developed close friendships with people who will join him at a moment's notice to see a good show. Most of all, Greenberg has done the thing that he most wanted to do, and he's gotten to do it on his terms: He plays the music he wants to hear and talks too much about it. For more than two decades, he's prioritized a hobby that allows him to have fun every week, to remain a "pure music nerd."

Greenberg has Thoreau-like devotion to his radio show. Just as Thoreau thought it was of highest importance to see a sunset each day. Greenberg thinks it's of the highest importance to get in front of his mic each week and play some music he loves. Will many people tune in? Hopefully. Does it matter? Not really. True fun is the point.

Care about the World

For Jodi Helmer, animal rescue began with a senior Great Dane named Binks, her first foster dog. Then Helmer fostered more dogs. Then cats. Then she and her husband, Jerry Porter, moved to a house on a couple of acres where they could get chickens, too.

Today, Helmer and her husband run Naughty Donkey Farm Sanctuary in Albemarle, North Carolina. They have about seventy dogs, cats, and farm animals, almost all of whom are special needs or hospice rescues. The tagline of the sanctuary is "Rescue. Rehabilitate. Spoil Rotten." When an animal arrives, Helmer promises it will spend the rest of its life getting the love and care it deserves. Her crew has included a blind donkey named Waylon and his best friend, Willy the rescue goat; a three-legged senior dog with cancer named Lt. Dan; and Benjamin Franklin, a turkey rescued from a poultry facility, who would follow people around like a puppy.

Helmer is a close friend. The reason I wanted to include her in this book is because I see how grueling this work is—emotionally, physically, and financially. I see how hard Helmer takes the loss of each animal—and when the animals come to her sanctuary with physical challenges or in old age, loss happens frequently. She does all of this on top of a full-time job. I wanted to learn from her: Is it worth it? The heartbreak? The around-the-clock care? To answer me, she shared the story of Seymour the Duck.

Seymour was born without eyes. Then, as a young duck, he suddenly lost the ability to walk. A blind, immobile duck is just the kind of animal that finds a home at Naughty Donkey Farm Sanctuary. A vet recommended euthanasia, but Helmer had an instinct this was wrong. She and her husband made him a duck-sized wheelchair, and soon, Seymour waddled around in his custom PVC walking machine. They even gave him water therapy to build his strength. One day, Seymour started walking again. Now he navigates his enclosure like a pro, playing with other special needs ducks and splashing in a kiddie pool.

"I see him out there every day, swimming in his pool and foraging and hanging out with his friends. I mean, he has friends!" Helmer gushed. "He has a pretty great life. If we had given up on him, he wouldn't have had that."

A few days before our conversation, Helmer had lost Walter the one-eyed hospice dog. Even through tears, she said she's committed to animal rescue. "It's emotionally taxing," she said. "Yet there's always a moment, at least one in each day, when I have an encounter with an animal or look out at them in the pasture and I think, 'This is it. This is the reason they deserve it.'"

AS IT COULD BE

Helmer shares an enviable trait with Thoreau: seeing the world as it could be, then realizing that they have the power to do something to bring their corner of the world closer to its ideal. I think this is the bravest and kindest way to live.

Thoreau lived a life that insisted on creating change. For six years, Thoreau refused to pay the part of his tax bill that would fund the Mexican-American War, and with it, the expansion of slavery. (Interestingly, Thoreau wasn't opposed to all taxes. He paid his highway tax, believing it was useful to his neighbors.) His refusal landed him in jail and inspired his essay, *Resistance to Civil Government*. The spoiler of this story is the unknown person who bailed Thoreau out against his wishes, ending his peaceful protest prematurely. (The prevailing theory is that it was a kindly aunt who hated the thought of her nephew in jail.)

But that one night in jail changed the world. Mahatma Gandhi said he was "greatly influenced" by Thoreau's act. Members of the Nazi resistance in Denmark used Thoreau's essay to develop their resistance strategy. Martin Luther King, Jr. was one of Thoreau's greatest admirers. He wrote,

> I became convinced that noncooperation with evil
> is as much a moral obligation as is cooperation

with good. No other person has been more elo-
quent and passionate in getting this idea across
than Henry David Thoreau. As a result of his writings and personal witness, we are the heirs of a legacy of creative protest. The teachings of Thoreau
came alive in our civil rights movement; indeed,
they are more alive than ever before.

WORTH THE SACRIFICE

Helmer's story also has a spoiler lurking in it, attempting to
bail her out of the good work she's doing. It's me. For the
first few years when Helmer and I met for monthly lunch
dates, I'd bite my lip to keep from telling her what I wanted
to tell her: Quit the sanctuary. No human can handle this
much heartbreak. I worried about her, and I wanted to find
a way to tell her to be more selfish without sounding like
a jerk.

This was unlike me. I used to be a do-gooder, a firm be-
liever in Muhammad Ali's philosophy that "service to others
is the rent you pay for the room here on earth." But things
took a turn about ten years ago. Political leaders embraced a
burn-it-all-down philosophy. Pundits had reason to use the
term "world war" with straight faces. Countries pulled out of
climate accords that were already insufficient for the task.
When the world risks self-inflicted catastrophes—political,

nuclear, environmental—do small acts of kindness even register? Is it better to just save yourself? I didn't understand how people like Helmer did it.

This wasn't my best me talking, of course. I wanted to be better. When I became the back-page columnist for *Charlotte* magazine in 2023, the editor asked how I wanted to focus my column. I was ready with my answer: "kind people doing good things quietly." I had a personal reason for this. I began to doubt how good it felt to do good. This was the homework I needed to get back to best-me.

Every month, I interview people who do good things without calling attention to themselves. No influencers taking selfies while they handed an unhoused person a sandwich. No leaders who volunteer with a public relations campaign. I talk with normal people who do good deeds: volunteers who furnish apartments and cook meals to welcome refugees who are new to town, a group who drives a mobile farmers market into underserved neighborhoods to give produce away, a woman who faces threats to run a desperately needed reproductive health care clinic. Thoreau wrote, "Be not simply good. Be good for something." I wanted to talk to the people who were good for something. And I, too, wanted to be good for something again.

None of these people had a surplus of time or money. They worked jobs, raised families, watched the same awful news that I did. I asked all of them what I asked Helmer: Why? Why do you do this? When the world seems to be falling apart, how do you empower yourself to take on this work? Each answered with a shrug and some version of "Because I have to help." What, to me, seemed like an act of superhuman hope, just seemed like the most obvious answer to them. They simply had to help.

Month by month, they cured me of my cynicism. I started doing more: volunteering to help immigrants find work in their chosen fields, making meals for people in shelters, fostering dogs, turning my yard into a wildlife habitat. I started to get it. Even as I became more attuned to the injustice around me, I became more aware of my power to do something about it. And I was better for it: less cynical, more hopeful, even empowered.

This effect has been well documented, from stories like *A Christmas Carol* to scientific research. A publication in the *International Journal of Behavioral Medicine* found "a strong correlation exists between the well-being, happiness, health, and longevity of people who are emotionally kind and compassionate in their charitable helping activities." The researchers even concluded that the healing powers of helping behaviors could be "prescribed" to improve public health.[7] Imagine what would happen if we all felt empowered to help and became happier by doing so. Imagine what would happen if we could envision the world as it could be and then use our lives to help bridge the real and the imagined.

Dr. Lakshmin cites two approaches to achieve an enjoyable life. The first is a hedonistic approach: finding happiness through pleasure. This might be a spa day, a movie night, a binge of our favorite show. It's hard to imagine a good life without hedonistic fun. Helmer's choice for hedonistic pleasure is the escapist fun of a formulaic book or movie. ("I know what the ending is going to be, and I like that," she said. "Because in animal rescue, you never know the ending.")

But, Dr. Lakshmin wrote, our lives wouldn't be complete without the other approach: eudaimonic pleasure:

> Eudaimonic well-being, in contrast, focuses on deriving meaning and having our actions be congruent with our values; it is the feeling that our lives are imbued with purpose. Instead of prioritizing pleasure or happiness, eudaimonic well-being emphasizes personal growth, acceptance of your authentic self, and connection to meaning."[8]

Hedonistic pleasure is ideal when you need a quick boost. But typically, after enjoying hedonistic pleasure, we return

to our usual emotional baseline. When we invest in eudaimonic pleasure, however, we can increasingly build our
emotional baseline over time. And when we steal minutes
from "fake fun," we can invest those minutes into the kind of
fun that makes a difference, both to ourselves and to others.

With the extra time his minimalist lifestyle gave him,
Joshua Becker of Becoming Minimalist founded an organization devoted to helping orphans. His organization, The
Hope Effect, places orphaned children in foster care with
families so they don't have to grow up in institutionalized
care. "While each of us is gifted with different passions, a different personality, and different capabilities," Becker wrote
in *Things That Matter*, "having a life lived with focus on the
things that matter most will always result in more accom-
plishments and fulfillment than we ever thought possible."

Even small acts of kindness result in big payoffs. After
the death of his wife, seventy-six-year-old Danny Chauvin
had little to fill his days. He's a Vietnam veteran in Missis-
sippi who has suffered with post-traumatic stress disorder,
and his mental health declined with all the grief and quiet.
He realized one of the things he missed about life with
his wife was checking off her honey-do list, so he posted
an offer on Facebook to check off other people's honey-do
lists. The requests flooded in—a broken closet door needed
to be fixed, a swing needed to be hung—mostly from single

or widowed women who call him "The Honey-Do Dude." He travels around town each day, doing these small projects for free. His PTSD has gotten much better since he began doing it. "Danny fixes the hole in his heart by fixing just about everything else," said Steve Hartman on a segment on CBS Evening News.

I find it inspiring that a life of purpose can be as simple as fixing someone's closet door or making a wheelchair for a duck. It's simply vital to join the people who do this work in big and small ways each day, helping animals, befriending the lonely, doing what one can—and refusing to support systems of injustice. Not only do these helpers connect our world, our heartbreaker of a world, closer to its ideal, but they get a little closer to becoming their ideal selves as well. They reap those Waldenomics earnings.

Thoreau cost himself friends and readers when he took strong abolitionism stands, especially with his support of John Brown. His family could've lost nearly everything they owned because of their work on the Underground Railroad. He freaked out his poor aunt when he went to jail. But without those beliefs and actions—without his focus on eudaimonic well-being in addition to his hedonist pleasures of nature—Thoreau just wouldn't be Thoreau. And, due to the contributions of those he inspired, we wouldn't be who we are today either.

Five Questions:
Embrace What Matters Most

1. If you could trim $100 a month in expenses—perhaps by resisting fast fashion or spontaneous purchases—how could you spend that money in a way that brought you greater Waldenomics profit? Consider the three main areas that give the most back: time with people, hobbies, and purpose.

2. Same question, but for time: If you created weeks of found time each year by minimizing "fake fun," how would you reallocate that time in a way that better serves you?

3. How did you cultivate the relationships that have meant the most to you?

4. Think of a neglected hobby, either one you stopped a while ago or one you haven't yet begun. How could affect your life if you invested time in it again?

5. Given your heart, mind, and talents, how can you make a difference in a way that few other people could?

NOTES

Introduction

1. Akilah Johnson and Charlotte Gomez, "Stress Is Weathering Our Bodies from the Inside Out," *The Washington Post*, October 17, 2023.

2. Brent Ranalli, "Laundry!" *The Concord Saunterer: A Journal of Thoreau Studies*, vol. 29 (2021): 12.

Chapter 1

1. Annabelle Timsit, "A Four-Day Workweek Pilot Was so Successful Most Firms Say They Won't Go Back," *The Washington Post*, February 21, 2023, *washingtonpost.com*.

2. Philip Van Doren Stern, ed. *The Annotated Walden* (Clarkson N. Potter, Inc., 1970), 107.

3. Joshua Becker, "How I Became Minimalist," Becoming Minimalist, September 10, 2024, *becomingminimalist.com/minimalist*.

4. "For Many People, Gathering Possessions Is Just the Stuff of Life," *Los Angeles Times*, March 21, 2014.

5. "Houses Are Still Big. Prices Are Much Bigger," *The New York Times*, August 17, 2023.

6. "A Fifth of Americans Rent Self Storage with Gen Xers In The Lead," StorageCafe, April 25, 2023.

7. Joshua Fields Millburn and Ryan Nicodemus, "Woodshedding and the Pseudo-Thoreau Thing: Moving to Montana," The Minimalists, rev. February 2013, *theminimalists.com*.

8. Joshua Fields Millburn and Ryan Nicodemus, *Everything That Remains* (Asymmetrical Press, 2014), 71.

9. Emily McFarlan Miller. "The Science of Sabbath: How People Are Rediscovering Rest—and Claiming Its Benefits," *Word&Way* January 2, 2019, *wordandway.org.*

10. Alex Kerai, "Cell Phone Usage Statistics: Mornings Are for Notifications," Reviews.org, July 21, 2023, *reviews.org.*

11. Susan Ratcliffe, ed. *Oxford Essential Quotations, 5th ed.* (Oxford Univeristy Press, 2017), *oxfordreference.com.*

12. Cal Newport, "The Year in Quiet Quitting," *The New Yorker*, December 29, 2022.

13. Kevin O'Leary, "'Quiet Quitting' Is a Cancer to Culture," LinkedIn, August 31, 2022.

14. Arianna Huffington, LinkedIn, August 16, 2022.

15. Jennifer Liu, "People Spend More than Half Their Day Doing Busy Work, According to Survey of 10,000-Plus Workers," CNBC, April 6, 2022, *cnbc.com.*

16. Katherine Tangalakis-Lippert, "The Back-to-Office Backfire: Companies Ending WFH Perks Lose Out on Top Talent, Who View Flexible Work as Equivalent to an 8% Raise," Business Insider, August 6, 2023, *businessinsider.com.*

17. Paolo Confino, "How Unpopular Are Return-to-Office Mandates? 99% of Companies Who Had One Saw a Drop in Employee Satisfaction, Study Finds," *Fortune*, January 26, 2024, *fortune.com.*

Chapter 2

1. Timothy Thorough, "How to Live—Mr. Thoreau's Example," *The New York Tribune*, April 7, 1849.

2. Anna Baluch," Average PTO in the US & Other PTO Statistics," *Forbes*, March 30, 2023, *forbes.com.*

3. Katie Mogg, "How Americans Learned to Stop Worrying and Take Vacation This Summer," *Wall Street Journal*, July 28, 2023, *wsj.com.*

4. "The Meditation Market Is Expected to Reach a Value of $14.6 Billion as per the Business Research Company's Meditation Global Market Report," *Glove Newswire*, June 29, 2023.

5. Jessica De Bloom, Sabine A. E. Geurts, and Michael A. J. Kompier, "Vacation (After-) Effects on Employee Health and Well-Being, and the Role of Vacation Activities, Experiences, and Sleep," *Journal of Happiness Studies* 14, no. 2 (2012): 613–33.

6. Cornelia Blank, et al. "Short Vacation Improves Stress-Level and Well-Being in German-Speaking Middle-Managers—A Randomized Controlled Trial," *International Journal of Research and Public Health* 15, no. 1 (2018): 130.

7. Stephen Kaplan, "The Restorative Benefits of Nature: Toward an Integrative Framework," *Journal of Environmental Psychology* 15, no. 3 (1995): 169–82.

8. Jennifer Shappley, "LinkedIn Members Can Now Spotlight Career Breaks on Their Profiles," LinkedIn, March 1, 2022.

9. Kira Schabram, Matt Bloom, and DJ DiDonna, "Research: The Transformative Power of Sabbaticals," *Harvard Business Review*, February 22, 2023.

10. Names and identifying characteristics have been changed to protect the family's privacy.

Chapter 3

1. Robert Sullivan, *The Thoreau You Don't Know: What the Prophet of Environmentalism Really Meant* (HarperCollins, 2009), 228.

2. Derek D. Rucker and Adam D. Galinsky, "Desire to Acquire: Powerlessness and Compensatory Consumption," *Journal of Consumer Research* 35, no. 2 (2008) 257–67.

3. Katie Pybus, "Income Inequality, Status Consumption and Status Anxiety: An Exploratory Review of Implications for Sustainability and Directions for Future Research," *Social Sciences & Humanities Open* 6, no. 1 (2022), *sciencedirect.com*.

4. Matt D'Avila, director. *The Minimalists: Less Is Now*. Netflix, 2021. 53 min. *www.netflix.com*

5. Robert Quillen, "Paragraphs," *Detroit Free Press* (Detroit, MI), June 4, 1928.

6. "Fashion for the Earth," Earthday.org, September 10, 2024, *earthday.org*.

7. "State of the Industry: Lowest Wages to Living Wages," The Lowest Wage Challenge, September 10, 2024, *lowestwagechallenge.com*.

8. "Austin, TX Rental Market," Zillow, September 10, 2024, *zillow.com*.

9. Ryan Ermey, "I love everything about it:' 38-Year-Old Only Spends $792 a Month to Live in a 160 Sq. Ft. RV," CNBC, December 28, 2023. *cnbc.com*.

10. Jonathon Jachura, "Top 35 Tiny Home Statistics and Facts of 2024," Today's Homeowner, December 27, 2023, *todays homeowner.com*.

11. A. Wilson and H. Wadham, "(Tiny) Spaces of Hope: Reclaiming, Maintaining, and Reframing Housing in the Tiny House Movement," *Environment and Planning D: Society and Space* 41, no. 2. (2023), 330–50.

Chapter 5

1. Arthur C. Brooks and Oprah Winfrey, *Build the Life You Want: The Art and Science of Getting Happier* (Portfolio/Penguin, 2024), 12..

2. Hanne K. Collins, "Relational Diversity in Social Portfolios Predicts Well-Being," *Proceedings of the National Academy of Sciences of the United States of America*, vol. 119, no. 43 (2022).

3. Bryce Ward, "Americans Are Choosing to Be Alone. Here's Why We Should Reverse That," *The Washington Post*, November 23, 2022.

4. S. D. Pressman et al., "Association of Enjoyable Leisure Activities with Psychological and Physical Well-Being," *Psychosomatic Medicine* 71, no. 7 (2009): 725–32.

5. T. F. Hughes, C. C. Chang, J. Vander Bilt, and M. Ganguli, "Engagement in Reading and Hobbies and Risk of Incident Dementia: The MoVIES Project," *American Journal of Alzheimer's Disease & Other Dementias* 25, no. 5 (August 2010): 432–8.

6. Lydia Saad, "Community, Hobbies and Money Grow in Importance to Americans," Gallup News, July 19, 2023, *gallup.com*.

7. S. G. Post, "Altruism, Happiness, and Health: It's Good to Be Good." *International Journal of Behavior Medicine* 12, no. 2 (2005): 66–77.

8. Pooja Lakshmin, *Real Self-Care: A Transformative Program for Redefining Wellness* (Viking, 2023).

BIBLIOGRAPHY

Becker, Joshua. *Things That Matter*. Waterbrook, 2022.

Burkeman, Oliver. *Four Thousand Weeks: Time Management for Mortals*. Farrar, Straus and Giroux, 2021.

Chaudhuri, Anita. "'We Have Brothers, Sons, Lovers—But They Can't Live Here!' The Happy Home Shared by 26 Women," *The Guardian*, August 24, 2023.

Chayka, Kyle. *Filterworld: How Algorithms Flattened Culture*. Doubleday, 2024.

Coleman, Daniel, and Richard J. Davidson. *Altered Traits: Science Reveals How Meditation Changes Your Mind, Brain, and Body*. Avery, 2017.

de Botton, Alain. *The Consolations of Philosophy*. Vintage Books, 2000.

de Botton, Alain. *Religion for Atheists: A Non-Believer's Guide to the Uses of Religion*. Vintage Books, 2012.

Emerson, Ralph Waldo. *Essays and Poems*. Everyman, 1996.

Ermey, Ryan. "I Love Everything About It:' 38-Year-Old Only Spends $792 a Month to Live in a 160 Sq. Ft. RV." CNBC, December 28, 2023.

Feiler, Bruce. *The Search: Finding Meaningful Work in a Post-Career World*. Penguin, 2023.

Ghodsee, Kristen R. *Everyday Utopia*. Simon & Schuster, 2023.

Hartman, Steve. "How a Vietnam Vet Found Healing as the 'Honey-Do Dude.'" CBS Evening News, February 2, 2024.

Henrich, Joseph. *The WEIRDest People in the World: How the West Became Psychologically Peculiar and Particularly Prosperous.* Farrar, Straus and Giroux. 2020.

Keillor, Garrison. "Meanwhile: September, Time to Lighten Up and Get a Grip." *The New York Times*, September 20, 2007.

Keller, Julia. *Quitting: A Life Strategy, The Myth of Perseverance—and How the New Science of Giving Up Can Set You Free.* Balance, 2023.

Khazan, Olga. *Weird: The Power of Being an Outsider in an Insider World.* Hachette Go, 2020.

Lakshmin, Pooja. *Real Self-Care: A Transformative Program for Redefining Wellness.* Viking, 2023.

Lamott, Anne. *Bird by Bird: Some Instructions on Writing and Life.* Anchor Books, 1995.

Lewis, Michael. "Obama's Way." *Vanity Fair*, October 2012.

Liming, Sheila. *Hanging Out: The Radical Power of Killing Time.* Melville House, 2023.

Mingyur Rinpoche, Yongey, and Helen Tworkov. *In Love with the World: A Monk's Journey Through the Bardos of Living and Dying.* Random House, 2019.

Newport, Cal. *Digital Minimalism: Choosing a Focused Life in a Noisy World.* Portfolio/Penguin, 2019.

Price, Catherine. *The Power of Fun: How to Feel Alive Again.* The Dial Press, 2021.

Reidhead, Julia, ed. *The Norton Anthology: American Literature, 1820-1865*, 7th Edition. Norton, 2007.

Searls, Damion, ed. *The Journal, 1837-1861: Henry David Thoreau.* New York Review of Books, 2009.

Schulz, Kathryn. "Pond Scum." *The New Yorker*, October 19, 2015.

Shulevitz, Judith. "Does Co-Housing Provide a Path to Happiness for Modern Parents?" *The New York Times*, October 22, 2021.

Stern, Philip Van Doren, ed. *The Annotated Walden*. Clarkson N. Potter, Inc., 1970.

Stolzoff, Simone. *The Good Enough Job: Reclaiming Life from Work*. Portfolio/Penguin, 2023.

Sullivan, Robert. *The Thoreau You Don't Know: What the Prophet of Environmentalism Really Meant*. HarperCollins, 2009.

Thompson, Derek. "Workism Is Making Americans Miserable." *The Atlantic*, February 24, 2019.

Thoreau, Henry David. *Walden, Everyman's Library Edition*. J.M. Dent Orion Publishing Group, 1995.

Thoreau, Henry David. *Walking & Life Without Principle*. CreateSpace, 2015.

Walls, Laura Dassow. *Henry David Thoreau: A Life*. The University of Chicago Press, 2017.

ABOUT THE AUTHOR

Jen Tota McGivney is a writer in Charlotte, North Carolina. She's the back-page columnist for *Charlotte Magazine*, and her work also appears in *SUCCESS Magazine*, *Our State Magazine*, and *Southern Living*, among others. She has a master's degree in English and a soft spot for the transcendentalists. *Finding Your Walden* is her first book.

McGivney lives with her husband, Jimmy, and their rescue pitties, Phoebe and Maddie.

To Our Readers

HAMPTON ROADS PUBLISHING, an imprint of Red Wheel/ Weiser, publishes inspirational books from a variety of spiritual traditions and philosophical perspectives for "the evolving human spirit."

Our readers are our most important resource, and we appreciate your input, suggestions, and ideas about what you would like to see published.

Visit our website at *www.redwheelweiser.com*, where you can learn about our upcoming books and also find links to sign up for our newsletter and exclusive offers.

You can also contact us at *info@rwwbooks.com* or at

Red Wheel/Weiser, LLC
65 Parker Street, Suite 7
Newburyport, MA 01950